Thomas James Mathias

The Pursuits of Literature

A Satirical Poem in Four Dialogues. Third Edition

Thomas James Mathias

The Pursuits of Literature
A Satirical Poem in Four Dialogues. Third Edition

ISBN/EAN: 9783337005771

Printed in Europe, USA, Canada, Australia, Japan

Cover: Foto ©Thomas Meinert / pixelio.de

More available books at **www.hansebooks.com**

THE

PURSUITS OF LITERATURE:

A

SATIRICAL POEM

IN DIALOGUE.

WITH NOTES.

Ουδ' αλαοσκοπιην ειχε κρε.ων Ενοσιχθων·
Και γαρ ὁ θαυμαζων ἡστο Πτολεμοντε Μαχηντε,
Υψυ επ' ακροτατης κορυφης Σαμυ ὑληεσσης
Θρηϊκιης, ενθεν γαρ εφαινετο πασα μεν Ιδη,
Φαινετο δε Πριαμοιο πολις, και νηες Αχαιων·
Αυτικα δ' εξ ορεος κατεβησατο παιπαλοεντος·
ΤΡΙΣ μεν ορεξατ' ιων, ΤΟ ΔΕ ΤΕΤΡΑΤΟΝ ἱκετο τεκμωρ
Αιγας, ενθα δε ὁι κλυτα δωματα ΒΕΝΘΕΣΙ ΛΙΜΝΗΣ
Χρυσεα μαρμαιροντα τετευχαται, αφθιτα αιει.

Hom. Il. 13. v. 10.

PART THE FOURTH AND LAST.

THE THIRD EDITION.

REVISED AND CORRECTED WITH MANY ADDITIONS.

LONDON:

PRINTED FOR T. BECKET, No. 81, PALL MALL.

1797.

Lately Published (price 1s. 6d.) A New Edition of

The IMPERIAL EPISTLE from KIEN LONG, Emperor of China, to GEORGE the Third, King of Great Britain, &c. &c. in the Year 1794. Transmitted from the Emperor, and presented to his Britannick Majesty by his Excellency the Right Hon. George Earl Macartney, of the Kingdom of Ireland, K.B. Ambassador Extraordinary and Plenipotentiary to the Emperor of China, in the Years 1792, 1793, 1794. Translated into English Verse from the Original Chinese Poetry. With notes by various Persons of Eminence and Distinction, and by the Translator.

Ignotum Rutulis Carmen cæloque Latino
Fingimus, et Finem egressi Legemque priorum.

N. B. It is thought proper to mention, that THE IMPERIAL EPISTLE is *not a burlesque Poem* in any sense of the word. But it is a POEM built upon the circumstances of the times, delineating the Characters of the Statesmen of Great Britain, with satire, pleasantry, or with praise; and exhibiting a picture of Europe at the period of its date. The whole is as the title implies conveyed under Chinese imagery and allusions, illustrated by references to original Writers, consistent with its Plan and Subject.

Printed for T. Becket, Pall-Mall.

ERRATUM.

In the Preface to the Third Part of the P. of L. page 8. l. 2. from the bottom, for " sufficient," read " insufficient."

ADVERTISEMENT

TO

THE FOURTH AND LAST PART

OF THE

PURSUITS OF LITERATURE.

L'OMBRA SUA TORNA CH'ERA DIPARTITA!   Dante.

"*Hear his speech, but say thou nought.*"
          " But one word more :—"
" *He will not be commanded!*"   Macbeth.

JUNE 1797.

AS I have now brought my Poem to the conclusion which I intended, it is proper and, as I think, respectful to offer some considerations to the public, for whose use it was written. No imitation of any writer or of any poem was proposed, except the adherence to the principles of juft composition and a *general* observation of the finished models of classical literature be considered as such. In the Preface to the Firft Part I said, what I now repeat, that I would not have printed it, but from a full conviction of it's *tendency* to promote the public welfare. My particular ideas on the nature and subject of SATIRE I expressed clearly and fully in the Advertisement to the Second Part, and under the influence and impreffion of those sentiments (a) I wrote the Poem. In my introduction to the Third Part, feeling the importance of my subject in it's various branches, I asserted that, " LITERATURE, *well or ill* " *conducted*, IS THE GREAT ENGINE *by which*, I am " fully persuaded, ALL CIVILIZED STATES *must ul-* " *timately be supported or overthrown.*" I am now

PART IV.   b   more

NOTE.

(a) Αλλοις κηρυξας, Αυτος αδοκιμος. Such is the condition of a Satirift.

more and more deeply impressed with this truth, if we
consider the nature, variety and extent of the word,
Literature. We are no longer in an age of ignorance,
and information is not partially distributed according to
the ranks, and orders, and functions, and dignities of
social life. All learning has an index, and every science it's abridgment. I am scarcely able to name any
man whom I consider as wholly ignorant. We no
longer look exclusively for learned authors in the usual
place, in the retreats of academic erudition and in the
seats of religion. Our peasantry now read the *Rights*
of Man on mountains and moors and by the way side;
and shepherds make the analogy between their occupa-
tion and that of their governors. Happy indeed, had
they been taught no other comparison. Our *unsexed*
female writers now instruct or confuse us and themselves in the labyrinth of politics, or turn us wild with
Gallic frenzy.

But there is one publication of the time too peculiar
and too important to be passed over in a general reprehension. There is nothing with which it may be compared.
A legislator in our own parliament, a member of the
House of Commons of Great Britain, an elected guardian
and defender of the laws, the religion, and the good manners of the country, has neither scrupled nor blushed to
depict and to publish to the world the arts of lewd
and systematic seduction, and to thrust upon the
nation the most open and unqualified blasphemy against
the very code and volume of our religion. And all this,
with his name, style, and title, prefixed to the novel or
romance called " THE MONK." (b) And one of our public theatres has allured the public attention *still more* to
this

NOTE.

"(b) " THE MONK, a Romance in 3 volumes by M.
LEWIS, Esq. M.P." printed for Bell, Oxford Street. At first
I thought that the name and title of the author were ficti-
tious, and some of the *public*-papers hinted it. But I have
been solemnly and repeatedly assured that it is the writing
and publication of M. LEWIS, Esq. *Member of Parliament.* It
is sufficient for me to point out Chap. 7, of Vol. 2. As a
composition the work would have been better, if the offensive

this novel, by a scenic representation of an Episode in it, not wholly uninteresting. *"O Proceres, Censore*

b 2 *opus*

NOTE.

sive and scandalous passages had been omitted, and it is disgraced by a *diablerie* and nonsense fitted only to frighten children in the nursery. I believe this 7th Chap. of Vol. 2. *is actionable at Common Law.* Edmund Curl in the first year of George II. was prosecuted by the Attorney General (Sir Philip Yorke afterwards Lord Hardwicke) for printing two obscene books. The Attorney General set forth the several obscene passages, and concluded, that *it was an offence a-gainst the King's peace.* The defendant was found guilty and set in the pillory.* See. Str. 788. 1 Barnardist 29. We know the proceedings against the *book,* entitled " Memoirs of a Woman of Pleasure," by John Cleland. To the passages of obscenity, (which certainly I shall not copy in this place) Mr. Lewis has added blasphemy against the Scriptures; *if* the following passage may be considered as such. " He (the Monk) examined the book which she " (Antonia) had been reading, and had now placed upon " the table. *It was* THE BIBLE. ' How,' said the Prior " to himself, ' Antonia reads the Bible, and is still so igno-" rant?' But upon further inspection he found that Elvira " (the mother of Antonia) had made exactly the same re-" mark. That *prudent* mother, while she admired *the beau-*" *ties* of THE SACRED WRITINGS, was convinced, that *unre-*

stricted,

NOTE ON THE NOTE.

* The indictment (in Mich. Term 1 G. II. begins thus: " EdmundCurl, *Existent homo iniquus et scelcratus nequiter machi-*" *nans et intendens bonos mores subditorum hujus regni corrumpere,*" *et eos adnequitiam inducere, quendam obscenum libellum intitu-*" *lat,*"&c.&c.—See Sir John Strange's Rep. p.777. Ed.1782. In *two or three days after* the point had been solemnly argued, and the judges had given their respective opinions, Sir J. Strange observes, " They gave it *as their unanimous opinion,* that *this was a temporal offence.*" And they declared also that if the famous case of the Queen against *Read* (6 Ann. in B. R.) was to be adjudged (*by them*) they should rule it *otherwise*; i. e. contrary to Lord Ch.J. Holt's opinion.—The Judges were Sir Robert (afterwards Lord) Raymond, Fortescue, Reynolds, and Probyn.

opus est, an Haruspice nobis?" I consider this as a new species of legislative or state-parricide. What is it to
                                                          the

---

N O T E.

" *stricted, no reading more improper could be permitted a young*
" *woman.* Many of the narratives *can only tend to excite*
" *ideas the worst calculated for a female breast*; every thing is
" called roundly and plainly by it's own name ; and *the an-*
" *nals of a brothel would scarcely furnish a greater choice of inde-*
" *cent expressions.* Yet this is the book which young wo-
" men are recommended to study, which is put into the
" hands of children, able to comprehend little more than
" those passages *of which they had better remain ignorant*, and
" *which but too frequently inculcate the first rudiments of vice, and*
" *give the first alarm to the still sleeping passions.* Of this
" Elvira was so fully convinced, that she would have *pre-*
" *ferred* putting into her daughter's hands Amadis de Gaul,
" or the Valiant Champion Tirante the White ; and *would*
" *sooner have authorised her studying the lewd exploits* of Don Ga-
" laor, *or the lascivious jokes* of the Damzel Plazer de mi vida."
(p. 247, 248.) &c. I state only what is printed. It is for
others to read it and to judge. The falshood of this passage
is not more gross than it's impiety. In the case of Thomas Woolston, in the 2d. of George II. for blasphemous discourses against our Saviour's miracles, when arrest of judgment was moved, Lord Raymond and the whole Court declared they would not suffer it to be debated, *whether* to
write against Christianity *in general* (not concerning contro-
verted points between the learned, but *in general*) was not an
offence punishable in the temporal Courts of Common Law.
Woolston was imprisoned one year, and entered into a
large recognizance *for his good behaviour during life.* Sir Philip Yorke, afterwards Lord Hardwicke, was Attorney General at the time. The case of the King against Annet,
when the Hon. Charles Yorke, was Attorney General, (3d
of Geo. III.) for a blasphemous book entitled " The Free
Inquirer," *tending*, among other points, to ridicule, *traduce*
and discredit the HOLY SCRIPTURES, is well known to the
profession. The punishment was *uncommonly* severe. Whether the passage I have quoted in a *popular* novel, has not *a*
tendency to corrupt the minds of the people, and of the youn-
                                                            ger

• Juv. Sat. 2.

the kingdom at large, or what is it to all those whose office it is to maintain truth, and to instruct the rising abilities and hope of England, that the author of it is *a very young man?* That forsooth he is a man of genius and fancy? So much the worse. That there are very poetical descriptions of castles and abbies in this novel? So much the worse again, the novel is *more alluring* on that account. Is this a time to poison the waters of our land in their springs and fountains? Are we to add incitement to incitement and corruption to corruption, till there neither is, nor can be, a return to virtuous action and to regulated life? Who knows *the age* of this author? I presume, very few. *Who does not know,* that he is a Member of Parliament? He has told us all so himself. I pretend not to know, (Sir John Scott does know, and practises too, whatever is honourable and virtuous and dignified in learning and professional ability) I pretend not, I say, to know, whether this be an object of parliamentary animadversion. Prudence may possibly forbid it. But we can feel that it is an object of moral and of national reprehension, when a Senator transgresses and violates his first duty to his (*d*) country. There are wounds and ob-

---

NOTE.

-ger unsuspecting part of the female sex, by *traducing and discrediting* THE HOLY SCRIPTURES, is a matter of public consideration.—" *This book goes all over the kingdom;*" are the words of Judge Reynolds, in the case of E. Curl. What Mr. LEWIS has printed *publicly with his name,* that I state publicly to the nation. Few will dissent from the opinion of Lord Raymond and the Court, in the case of Curl above stated, as reported by Strange and Barnardiston to this effect; " Religion is *part of the common law,* and therefore *whatever* " *is an offence* against that, is an offence *against* THE COMMON " LAW." With this *opinion,* I conclude the note.

(*d*) All members of the legislature, Peers or Commoners, should join in sentiment and in character with the Athenian orator, and be considered as speaking to their country in these words: " Ημεις, οις ιερα και ταφοι προγονων υπαρ- " χησιν εν τη Πατριδι, και διατριβαι, και συνηθειαι μεθ' " ὑμων ελευθεροι, και γαμοι κατα τας νομας, και κηδεσται, " και

obstructions and diseases in the political, as well as in the natural, body, for which the removal of the part affected is alone efficacious. At an hour like this, are we to stand in consultation on the remedy, when not only the disease is ascertained, but the very stage of the disease and it's specific symptoms? Are we to spare the sharpest instruments of authority and of censure, when public establishments are gangrened in the life-organs?

I fear, if our legislators are wholly regardless of such writings and of such principles *among their own members*, it may be said to them, as the Roman Satirist said to the patricians of the empire, for offences slight indeed, when compared to these.

" *At vos*, Trojugenæ, *vobis ignoscitis, et quæ*
Turpia cerdoni Volesos Brutosque *decebunt.* (e)

There is surely something peculiar in these days; something wholly unknown to our ancestors. But men, however dignified in their political station, or gifted with genius and fortune and accomplishments, may at least be made ashamed, or alarmed, or convicted before the tribunal of public opinion. Before that tribunal, and to the law of reputation, and every binding and powerful sanction by which that law is enforced, is Mr. LEWIS this day called to answer.

But to return. The objects of public regret and offence are *now* so numerous and so complicated, that all the milder offices of the Muse have lost their influence and attraction. It is indeed unfortunate that scarce a subject in literature can be interesting without the science and matter of politics.(*f*)They give a colour to our very thoughts. We are borne down with a force not to be

re-

N O T E.

" και τεκνα, αξιοι της ὑμετερας πιστεως. κτλ. Æschin: περι Παραπρεσβειας. Sect. 11.

(*e*) Juv. Sat. 8. v. 181.

resisted, when our very existence, as a nation under its ancient

---

NOTE.

(*f*) "Quibus *occupatus et obsessus* animus quantulum loci bonis artibus relinquit!" Dialog. de Oratoribus C 29.—I cannot resist giving an opinion at *this* time. My prime objection to any proposed Ministry of Mr. Fox and his adherents is this. I believe their principles are *too popular* for the good, the safety, or perhaps for the existence, of this country under it's present constitution: I believe, that their design is to throw such a weight of power into the house of Commons, *by means of a Reform*, as *would* ultimately mould *the two* Houses of Parliament not merely into a resemblance, but into the actual form and relative power of the Council of Five Hundred and the Council of Ancients; and I am of opinion, that the authority and influence of the Crown of Great Britain would be reduced far below that which is lodged in the Executive Directory of France. I think the proposed Reforms *lead*, beyond a controversy, *to this issue.* I am of opinion that a great Personage, in the case of a change of Mr. Pitt's Ministry, must be apprehensive, *to whom* he is to be delivered, and *to what* he may be reduced. *The pride* of a statesman's understanding, like Mr. Fox's, in the plenitude of dignity will overbear all ideas of a balance of power in the orders of the state and of the safety of the country upon it's ancient principles. He has declared his opinion; he must not recede. All will be sacrificed *to that pride* in a moment of phrenzy. The example of every state, nation, and city, subdued by French arms, French principles and French treachery, is to be weighed well, as an aweful warning *in this* kingdom, which may *yet* be preserved. The *encroachments of such* a statesman, as Mr. Fox, (paramount as he is in ability and in *political* eloquence beyond any man) are to be watched and resisted by all who think soberly, and are independent of party. Yet Mr. Fox neither could nor would satisfy the raving and tyrannical ideas of Horne Tooke and the French crew. They would make use of him to a certain point. They would *then* declare him an enemy to his country, and conduct him to the scaffold. "Corpora lentè augescunt, CITO *extinguuntur.*"§ The security of property, public and private, is shaken by the proposed system, and a Revolution, (which

---

§ Tacit. Agric. ap. init.

ancient laws and constitution and establishments, has been rendered dubious. A man of a poetical mind either

wanders

NOTE.

we never *yet* have known but in mere name) might then be at hand. A government, which once relaxes, is not easily *recalled* to the vigour of it's ancient principles. We have statesmen of determined and of true patriotism, and this final misery may yet be prevented. We have a King, who has courage, virtue, and firmness. Of his Minister, the Right Hon. Wm. Pitt, I have given my opinion often *in another place*; I have not altered my sentiment. I certainly cannot say with the great satirist under Louis the 14th,

" Que ma vüe à COLBERT inspiroit l'allégresse." §

I speak, and I have spoken, impartially of MR. PITT. I am neither for a proscription of any political talents, nor for an hereditary claim to the public office of Prime Minister. But if the principles of any statesman are such as to induce a *real and effectual change* in the government, that statesman should not be admitted to rule. If the ancient and established principles of the English constitution are maintained, a Prime Minister may conduct public affairs even with a mediocrity of talent. It is neither Mr. Pitt, nor Lord Lansdown, nor Mr. Fox, nor Mr. Grey, who are necessary to the function. But, by the disastrous consent of the whole nation and it's Parliament, thinking rightly, proposing soundly, and meaning honestly, are nothing *without* SPEAKING WELL.—Let me add a word or two on a subject not quite foreign to this note.—The example of a very learned and, in my opinion, of a very virtuous and honourable man, to whom the country is under some obligation, MR. REEVES, will deter any man from *volunteer effusions* in favour of any Minister. It would not be amiss, to be sure, if Mr. R. or any other writer would read Quintilian on tropes and metaphors, before he adorns his native language with all the richness of imagery, and exerts the command, which nature gives him, over *the figures* of speech. *Trunco, non frondibus, efficit umbram.* For my own part, when his pamphlet " The Thoughts on the English Government" was published, I never felt more indignation than when I saw this gentleman ungenerously and shamefully abandoned and given up by Mr. Pitt in the H. of Commons to the malice of

his

§ Boileau Ep. 10.

wanders into futurity, or recals the images of other
times and of other empires. He can sometimes even de-
.scend

---

his avowed enemies, and to a criminal prosecution in the
Court of King's Bench. He was solemnly acquitted of any
libellous intention; but his language was imprudent. He
fell a victim to metaphorical luxuriance and state-botany.
—(See "Thoughts &c." as above, pag. 12 and 13 for Mr.
Reeves's Simile of *the Constitutional Tree and it's Branches*.)

. I will propose another subject for consideration.—If any
man would peruse the acount given by *Thucydides* of the *democratic sedition* in Corcyra; (Book 3.) he would be convinced that
the same peculiarities mark all popular seditions and insurrec-
tions, the same pretexts, the same motives. The insurgents
declare the friends of the lawful and established government enemies to the popular representation and interest.
Some of these insurgents have private enmities to revenge,
and others have debts to cancel: death is the universal sol-
vent. Hear the great Historian: " Τ*ην μεν αιτιαν επιφε-
ροντες τοις του Δημον καταλυησιν. Απεθανον τινες ιδιας εχθρας
ἑνεκα, και αλλοι χρηματων σφισιν οφειλομενων ὑπο των λα-
βοντων.*Sect. 81. The historian observes, they held forth either
the specious offer of greater *equality of power among the citizens,*
or a more temperate form of *aristocracy,* or some state-
expedient varying with the hour; but each leader in reality
had his own private views of ambition, or power, or riches,
but accommodated his speeches to the prevailing humour of
the day. Hear him again in his own language. ' " Ο*ι εν
ταις πολεσιν προσταντες μετ' ονοματος ἑκαστοι ευπρεπης, πλη-
θης Ισονομιας πολιτικης, και Αριστοκρατιας σωφρονος προ-
τιμησει, τα μεν κοινα λογω θεραπευοντες αθλα εποιυντο, παν
τι δε τροπω αγωνιζομενοι αλληλων' περιγιγνεσθαι·—και η
μετα ψηφη αδικη καταγνωσεως,η χειρι κτωμενοι το κρατειν
ετοιμοι ησαν την αυτικα Φιλονεικιαν εμπιμπλαναι.*"lb. Sect. 82.
This, as we have all known, has been transacted step
by step upon a great and tremendous scale in France.
The Italian and Belgian states are following them
with headstrong and infuriate revolution. WE have indeed MORE TO PRESERVE THAN ANY OTHER COUNTRY
under heaven, and we may, by wise regulations, hereafter
restore even the finances of the state. We must *never* forget that the stability of our present Constitution is the sole

PART IV.   c   : stability

scehd into the regions of terrific fable, and give to his own country the sentiments and passions of antiquity, and body forth contending parties which are no more, of the virtuous and the valiant, of the wicked the desperate and the frantic. At such an hour as the present, and with the objects which we see and hear and feel, with the exultation of the bad, and the dejection of the good, and the labours of great statesmen *to preserve us from final misery*, can we forbear to contemplate the picture drawn by that poet, whose only Muses were Cæsar, and Brutus, and Cato, and the genius of expiring Rome.

Tristis FELICIBUS UMBRIS
Vultus erat; vidi Decios natumque patremque,
Lustrales bellis animas, *flentemque* Camillum.
Abruptis Catilina minax fractisque catenis
Exultat, Mariique truces nudique Cethegi :
Vidi ego lætantes, popularia nomina, Drusos
Legibus immodicos, ausosque ingentia Gracchos.
Æternis chalybum nodis, et *carcere Ditis*
Constrictæ plausere manus, CAMPOSQUE PIORUM
POSCIT TURBA NOCENS! *(g)*

Luc. L. 6. v. 784..

The

NOTE.

stability of all property, public and private. I speak from awful and trembling conviction, OUR RUIN CAN BE EFFECTED BY POLITICAL REFORM ALONE, and our Enemies at home and in France know that I speak the truth. We in Great Britain, who are *yet* in a condition to preserve ourselves, see and read and feel these things. The grant of *one demand* leads necessarily to another when any material alteration in a state or government is conceded. If the second is refused after the first has been granted, we are then told, that there is a want of consistence in the plan, and that it were more adviseable to have kept the state as it was, than to admit only a partial reform. We surely cannot be said to be *duped* and *fooled* by Reformers without warning from history and from experience. The *constitutional* statesmen of Great Britain cannot *now* be ignorant of the nature of " *a Modern Reform in any* " *state of Europe.*" The greater the difficulty and danger, the greater the fury of the Revolutionists. Pindar was a poet and a stateman; he said: Απροσικτων Ερωτων οξυτεραι μανιαι.
(Nem. Od. 11.)

The present Poem was not composed for a trivial purpose, or without mature thought. It is the fruit and study,

---

N O T E.

(g) In the great question of a Reform in Parliament (i. e. in the House of Commons) I certainly do not mean to call figuratively the ministerial ground, the *Campi Piorum*, but I call the Constitution of England and it's defenders in or out of Parliament by that name. Nor would I by any means rank the gentlemen of opposition with the *Turba nocens*. That *turba nocens* are the levellers and the partisans of democracy and revolution. But the licence of poetry we are told is considerable, if assumed with *modesty*. The question itself has nothing to do with invention, though I think much *fiction* is employed in the support of it. I am of opinion, that in the outset there is a fiction or a deceit. We are told we must recur to the *original* principle of the H. of C. the principle, as I suppose, on which it was founded, and that principle is declared to be *popular*, in the *modern* sense of that word. In this argument historical truth is not asserted; I would maintain, that it is violated. It is contrary to matter of fact. The very origin of the House itself (the best antiquaries will tell you so) is rather doubtful. The more remote your enquiry, the greater the demonstration of it's *original* weakness, nay (I say it with grief) of it's political insignificance. It was a Council, which grew out of a greater Council, and it was designed to represent *the property* of the kingdom. I will not insult my reader with information on the subject. But it is matter of plain historical knowledge that it's powers, it's functions, it's freedom, and it's consequence have been all *progressive* to a certain period. That period was the Revolution (as it is foolishly called) in 1688. At that æra the House of Commons *under the Old Whigs*, attained to the consummation of it's glory and to the fulness of it's dignity. As I here speak of the *original* principle, I have nothing to do with the subsequent corruptions. I must own I do not wish for the famous Roman plate of brass; I am for no unqualified Lex Regia. †

NOTE ON THE NOTE.

† See a Dissertation " de Ænea Tabula Capitolina Romæ 1757." Heineccius and Gravina also published this " Lex Regia." It may be read at full length in Gruteri Inscript: Antiq. By this Law the Roman Senate in the most abject stile *authorised* Vespasian *to make and repeal laws*, to

declare

study of an. independent and disinterested life, passed
without the incumbrance of a profession or the embar-
rassment

NOTE.

Let it rest in the Capitoline Museum, that splendid effort
of Michael Angelo. I abhor abject servility and all it's
monuments. I never wished, I am sure I do not now
wish, to see *any* Senate divest itself of all power. I would
not see a *Vespasian* in any country *make and repeal* laws, or
exercise *unlimited* authority without the advice and consent
of a well-constituted Senate. I venerate the institution of
the House of Commons, and would preserve it with my life ;
but I shall raise up no tree, trunk or branches, for a fatal
simile, like Mr. Reeves. I look for no pasture in the fields
of Ministers or of Booksellers ; nor would I be turned out
by Mr. Fox and Mr. Sheridan to graze on the verdant lawns
of the King's Bench with the Chief Justice of Newfound-
land, or at best in Mr. Pitt's *Strawyard*. I neither recur to
Montesquieu nor to Machiavel. I want not to be told by
the former that " *our* system was found in the woods," or
to hear from Signor Machiavel and Mr. Fox, that " *States
" may grow out of shape.§*" For my own part, I would rather
find

NOTE ON THE NOTE.

declare peace and war, and to exercise *every act* of an *absolute*
sovereign, without waiting for their consent or even ask-
ing their advice.—This authority however was not granted
to all the Emperors indiscriminately ; they *selected* (before
Vespasian) Augustus, Tiberius, and Claudius. I leave the
reader to his own reflections.

§ The words of Machiavel quoted by Mr. Fox in the H:
of C. on May 26, 1797, in his speech on the Reform of
Parliament. The founders of the French Republic, and the
Re-founders of it (for it has been *founded three times* already)
seem *always* to have had Machiavel's Discourses on Livy in
their view. He says, that if *any* power or powers, (princes,
warriors, or demagogues) take or subdue any city, province,
or realm, " *they should make all things new in the state.*" The
words are most particular. " Fare ogni cosa *di nuovo* in
" quello stato, nelle Città fare *nuovi governi con nuovi nomi,*
" con nuova autorità, con nuovi uomini, *fare i poveri ricchi,*
" disfare delle vecchie città, cambiare gli abitatori da un
" luogo ad un altro, e in somma, non lasciare *cosa niuna in-*
" *tatta,* e che non via sia *nè grado,nè ordine, nè stato, né richez-*
" *za,* che chi la tiene non la RICONOSCA DA TE !" Machiav.
Discorsi Lib.1. Cap. 6: The French have *religiously* observed
the advice. *We* are told in the H: of C. by Mr. Fox that the
authority of Machiavel is great. In my opinion, ALL
TYRANNY *is uniform in it's maxims.*

rassment of business. It was not intended merely to raise a smile at folly or conceit; but it was written with indignation

---

N O T E.

find a system in the woods, than in modern France; and I do not look for *a new political Dancing Master* every time there is a twist in the body. To hear Mr. Fox, as I *perpetually* do in the House, one would really think he was a rival to Vestris or Didelot. He has been long trying his art and giving lessons to Mr. Pitt *gratis*. That Right Honourable Gentleman's gait still continues as aukward and stiff as usual. He will not BEND. *A graceful bow* is not his ambition, and Mr. Fox *dances* before him every day *without the least effect*. Mr. Fox, I believe, is of the opinion and principle of Monsieur Marcel, the famous *dancing master* in Queen Anne's reign, who said, when the Earl of Oxford was made Prime Minister, " He was surprised, and could not tell what the Queen could see in him, for his own part *he never could make any thing of him*." To be sure Mr. PITT is every day placed *between* THE DANCING MASTER AND HIS MAN, but he has not yet learned *grace* from Mr. Fox, or *wit* from Mr. Sheridan. Indeed I have been informed that, the three celebrated *Dancers* and Ballet Masters, Messrs. Fox, Sheridan and Grey, are preparing a *new Serious Divertissement*, or Pas de Trois, with *new scenes, dresses* and *decorations*, called, " LE DIRECTOIRE EXECUTIF." If it can be *got up* time enough, it will be *brought forward this season*; but as there is a necessity for a re-inforcement of *the troop* FROM PARIS, it is feared *the old dances* must continue to the end of this season. June 1797. It is proposed that *light* should be thrown *on the stage* in a *quite new* manner; but the Ballet-Masters will suffer no persons to be on the stage, or to view the machinery *behind the scenes*. Lord Galloway and Lady Mary Duncan have expressed their approbation of this rule, so much for the interest of THE GRAND OPERA: though the noble Earl is contented with *the present Grand Ballet-Master.*—As I have no place so convenient for them, I beg leave to offer a few words on a subject, *now* peculiarly interesting. The time is my excuse. In the *impending* negociation for peace with the French (June 1797) it is not unpleasant or foreign to the subject to recollect the orations of the two great Athenians Demosthenes and Æschines, Περι Παραπρεσβειας, or *De Falsa Legatione*. Lord Malmsbury's present Embassy, (I hope not, like the last, a Παραπρεσβεια) will be conducted,

indignation against wickedness, against the prostitution
of superior talents, and the profane violence of bad men.

It

---

as I trust, upon strong principles, and *reported* in a different
mode from the former. *By knowing where to stand*, Philosophers and Statesmen have shaken the moral and political
universe. Lord Malmsbury's Letter to Lord Grenville
concerning his conversation with Mons. Charles Delacroix,
(I do not mean *any other* part of the correspondence)
was published by the most indiscreet advice, and in violation of every principle of diplomatic prudence. One would
think the Ministers published it to shew how *prettily and*
wittily their Ambassador could write, in defiance of all discretion and sound judgment. It reminds us of what Demosthenes accused his colleague in that famous Legation.
I cannot enter into particulars; I suppose knowledge in
most of my readers. The words are indeed remarkable
in their application; the party accused, Æschines himself
has recorded them. " Απολωλεκεναι Με⁻(εφη) την Πολιν
και τυς Συμμαχυς· και ειρετο με, ει των Αθηνησι πραγμα-
των επιλελησμαι, και τον Δημον καταπεπονημενον και σφοδρα
επιθυμυντα ΤΗΣ ΕΙΡΗΝΗΣ ει μεμνημαι." But most specifically and in the most appropriated manner, when he
urged against Æschines the imprudence of his language :
Ουτω ηρεθικας Φιλιππον και τοσαυτα ειρηκας, εξ ων υκ
Ειρηνη γενοιτ' αν εκ Πολεμυ, αλλ' εξ Ειρηνης Πολεμος α-
κηρυκτος." Æschin. Περι Παραπρεσβ. Sect. 16. p. 26. Edit.
Brooke, Oxon. 1721. One would think the words were
written for the late occasion. I hope Lord Malmsbury will
now adapt his language and his *dispatches* with more prudence to *Philip* and *the Directory*.—On a kindred topic I
would observe to the classical reader another *singular* circumstance in ancient times. It is from the Roman state.
Since we have all been arming at home with alacrity and
prudence, and (what is consequent to that) with effect,
against OUR enemy, and the militia laws have been exten-
ded, it is curious to call to mind *the emphatic clause* in the
ancient Roman law concerning *the exemption* of particular
persons from military service, called " DE VACATIONE,"
as learned Civilians well know. The Clause is this: " *Ni-*
" *si* BELLUM GALLICUM *exoriatur*;" in which case not even
the Priests were exempted. I will illustrate this law
from Plutarch and Cicero, but I will not translate the passages.

It was indeed (to use a poet's allusion) poured forth as a libation from the cup of Achilles, consecrated and appropriated :

Ουτε τεω σπενδεσκε θεων, οτε μη ΔΙΙ Πατρι. (h)

It is proposed, in it's degree and according to it's subject, for the defence of truth, and with an honest wish to uphold society and the best interests of mankind, but chiefly those of our own country. In it there are no
imaginary

N O T E.

ges In the life of Marcellus, Plutarch has this singular remark : " Ου μην αλλα μεγαν η τε χωρα παρειχε φοβον, δια την γειτνιασιν, ομορω και προσοικω πολεμω συνοισομενοις, και το παλαιον αξιωμα των Γαλατων· (the Gauls or *French*) ους μαλιστα Ρωμαιοι δεισαι δοκουσιν, ατε δη και την Πολιν υπ' αυτων αποβαλοντες, εξ εκεινου δε θεμενοι Νομον, ατελεις ειναι στρατειας τους Ιερεας, πλην ει μη Γαλατικος παλιν επελθοι Πολεμος. Εδηλου δε και τον φοβον αυτων η τε Παρασκευη. Μυριαδες γαρ εν οπλοις αμα τοσαυται Ρωμαιων ουτε προτερον ουτε υστερον γενεσθαι λεγονται." Plut. Vit. Marcel. p. 244. Vol. 2 Edit. Bryan.—The other illustration is from Cicero in his oration for Fonteius; (the object of which was to inculcate, " Gallis fidem non habendam, hominibus levibus, perfidis, et in ipsos Deos immortales impiis.")the words are these: " *Ut oportet*, BELLO GALLICO, ut majorum jura " moresque præscribunt, NEMO EST, Civis Romanus, *qui* " *sibi ulla excusatione utendum putet.*" Orat. pro Fonteio. Sect. 16. sub. fin. Cic. Op. Ed. Barbou. Vol. 4. p. 393.—We have not, and I trust we never shall have, *the same* cause for apprehension from the French as the Romans had from the Gauls. *They never have taken* OUR CITY, and while we are true to ourselves, *as we now are*, they never will or can take it. But the danger is and ever will be great, *from their vicinity*, δια την γειτνιασιν. The words are from Plutarch: Mr. Burke has written the commentary.‡ " *Vocem adyti dignam* " *templo !*"

(h) Hom. Il. 16. v. 227.

‡ Two Letters on the Peace. (Ed. Rivington 1796.) pag. 113, &c.

imaginary subjects. I have raised no phantoms of absurdity merely to disperse them ; but the words, the
works, the sentiments and often the actions of the authors are before us. It might be known *hereafter* from
this poem how we wrote and thought in this age, and not
unfrequently how we conducted ourselves.

There is one subject which I have pressed upon the
attention of the nation, which in this respect seems to
be in a state between slumber and alarm ; in the supine-
ness which attends the former, and with that confusion
in ideas and measures which too frequently accompanies
terror. Compassion, mercy, self-preservation, integrity of principle, Christian charity, the uncertainty of
the mortal condition, the convulsion of empires and of
states, have all and each variously conspired to direct the
measures of our government with respect to the French
Roman Catholic Emigrants, and in particular, to the
French Priests. I have stated in different places my
opinion on this important subject. I continue to call
aloud upon this country and it's ministers to regard, *with
minute circumspection*, THESE MEN AND THEIR CAUSE.
The most reprehensible part of Mr. Burke's public conduct has been in this point. Great and venerable as I hold
him, in this I praise him not. I maintain that the vigilance
of the Roman Catholics is erect and on the tiptoe of expectation : it is scarcely suspended by slumber. I speak also on
another account. There is such a connection between
superstition and atheism, and their allies cruelty and tyranny, that the wisest and most experienced statesmen
and moralists have declared it to be indissoluble. In *their*
cause, they would unite with any, even with Jacobin, principles. Hear Dr. Hussey the titular Bishop of Waterford
in Ireland in his late pastoral Letter.† " THE CATHO-
LIC FAITH (i. e. the tenets, the doctrines, the supersti-
tions, the absurdities, the follies, the cruelty, and the
tyranny, of the Church of Rome, and whatever makes it
to

NOTE.

(*a*) See "A Pastoral Letter to the Catholic Clergy of Waterford and Lismore in Ireland, by the R. R. Doctor Hussey" London *Re*printed by P. Coghlan, Duke Street, Grosvenor

to differ from any other *external* establishment of Christianity) *The Catholic faith* (says his *titular* Lordship) is suitable to *all* climes, and *all* forms of government, monarchies or *republics*, aristocracies, or DEMOCRACIES."

(p. 9.)

NOTE.

venor Square. 1797. His *titular* Lordship's idea of " a man of true liberality is this; " that he lives in charity, in concord, in amity, with *all others* of *every* religious persuasion; with whom a difference in religious opinions makes *no* difference in social life, &c, &c." (p. 6.) Very liberal indeed; this is the text. But his Lordship, in the natural confusion of ideas in *his* country has *prefixed* the comment. See *the preceding* page. The words are these: " Remonstrate (says " his Lordship) with any parent, who will be *so criminal* " as to *expose* his offspring to *those places of education* (the " Charter Schools &c. &c. as I suppose) where *his religious* " *faith and morals* are likely to be perverted. *If he will not at-* " *tend* to *your* remonstrances, (he is speaking to the Roman " Catholic Clergy) *refuse him* the participation of Christ's " body; *if* he should *still* continue *obstinate*, DENOUNCE " HIM TO THE CHURCH, in order that, according to Christ's " commandment, *he be considered as a heathen and a publican.*" page 5. We know the sense of Christ; and we know *the sense which the* ROMAN CATHOLIC CHURCH annexes to *these words.*" But this is LIBERALITY!!!—In Ireland it might be of use to discuss this pastoral Letter *in toto.* If I were an Irishman, I would do so: but the business in England is *yet* very different. Let me add a word or two. It may be worth while at *this* period when all establishments are shaking, to consider frequently, that " a Re- " ligious Establishment, under any form, is not the religion " itself, but the mode of preserving, inculcating, and con- " tinuing the religion.". There is a religion which may be and is political, and another which is real. I will give a passage from the admirable Preface to the translation of Xenophon's Cyropædia written with great compass of thought and precision of argument, by a gentleman of fortune, family, erudition and virtue, *the Hon.* MAURICE ASHLEY. I cannot refrain from observing with pleasure, that LORD MALMSBURY *and myself* may have a *natural* partiality for the memory of that accomplished and well-instructed gentleman. " Real Christianity (says he) is none of " all these changeable establishments and human institu- " tions, nor ever can be, *but stands upon its own foot.* " Whether it be the religion of the multitude, and national " or not national, or whatever be the forms of it in national

(p. 9.) Right. Flectere si nequeunt superos *Acheronta* movebunt. That which is true of Christianity *in itself and by itself alone*, independent of *any* establishment whatsoever, that they assert of their own tyrannical superstition. They will shew the arm and the sword of heaven interested and active *for them*. They will tell you, (whenever they have the power or even the probability of attaining that power) that their cause alone is from above. They separate *their* spiritual rulers from the temporal governors of the state, and assert the superior dignity and paramount authority of the former; and this they thunder in the ears of an armed soldiery. They tell you, that the opposers of the Roman Catholic cause are sacrilegious in the eye of heaven; and that upon them, in a mass, THE GREAT STONE will fall and grind them to powder. I know the state of Ireland,† and the declarations of

---

NOTE.

" establishments, *is one and the same in itself*, firm and unal-
" terable, and will undoubtedly remain so *to the end of the*
" *world*, whether owned or not owned by any public esta-
" blishment indifferently." Mr. A's Pref. pag. 8. I enter not into the expedience, institution and relative excellence of religious establishments in this place. It is not here the question; if it were, I am not without my sentiments or without words to enforce them. I hope indeed we may and shall *still* justify the expressions of a great writer: " *We are* " *separated from the errors and freed from the chains of* " POPERY *without breaking out into a state of religious anarchy.*" But I give Mr. Ashley's words as *a general* observation to *all* those who esteem the downfall of *such* an establishment as *Popery* to be the downfall of the Christian religion, than which no opinion can be more unfounded. To the Roman Catholic *system* of religion, whether in it's vigour and plenitude of power, or in its decline, or *in it's struggles for revival*, the words of the poet may be applied figuratively and literally:

In *sua* templa *furit*, nullâque exire vetante
Materiâ, magnamque *cadens* magnamque *revertens*
Dat *stragem* latè, SPARSOSQUE RECOLLIGIT IGNES.
LUC.L. 1.

† There is something *peculiarly ungrateful* in the conduct of this *titular* Bishop of Waterford. Particular attention has been paid to Dr. Hussey by the administration of Ireland, as Lord Camden knows. But in *this* country I should hardly be understood if I were to enumerate the particulars *which I know. I* have spoken in terms very moderate indeed of this Pastoral Letter *under the circumstances of* it's publica-

of the *titular* bishops in that country. But that subject is not properly mine, though it is intimately connected with it. All I have to do is to shew, (and I think I have shewn it to all who will attend,) that " *the Spirit of the Roman-Catholic System is yet unaltered.*" In England the French Priests, in a body, have been chased from the Kings Castle at Winchester: but our government has yet a sacred fortress or two at Reading, and Shene and in Yorkshire; and it appears that a sum of FIVE HUNDRED AND FORTY THOUSAND POUNDS (*b*) has been issued for the use of the French Emigrants, *sacred and profane*, in the course of the year 1796. This is ratified by the vote of Parliament. On this particular topic I shall say nothing further in this place. (*c*)

The

NOTE

tion. My reprehension has been confined *to the spirit of it.* It will be perceived by *some* persons that I write Συνετοισι.

Talibus *ex adyto* dictis CUMÆA SIBYLLA
Horrendas canit ambages, antroque remugit
Obscuris vera involvens !

(*b*) On the 21st Dec. 1796, " The House of Commons in " a Committee of Supply, among other sums, voted a sum " of 540,000l. for the relief of the suffering clergy and laity " of France." Woodfall's Parliamentary Register. 1796. Vol. I. page 524. It is singular (and it will be remembered by those who are versed in the interior politics of this country in the reign of Queen Anne) that in Swift's Examiner Nov. 1710, No. 16. the *exact sum* of 540,000l. is stated humorously, as " *a Bill of British ingratitude,*" to his Grace the Duke of Marlborough. viz. " Woodstock 40,000l. Blenheim, 200,000l. Post Office grant 100,000l. Mildenheim 30,000l. pictures, jewels, &c. 60,000l. Pall Mall grant &c. 10,000l. Employments &c. 100,000l. The Total *exactly* 540,000l." Thus at the beginning of this century did the British nation remunerate THE CONQUEROR OF FRANCE! *And thus*, at the close of it, are *the Services* of the French Emigrants, *sacred and profane*, annually *requited* by the munificence of the British Parliament!!! We know where it is written in letters of marble;

EUROPÆ HÆC VINDEX GENIO DECORA ALTA BRITANNO!

(*c*) I have just seen another production of a *Roman Catholic Divine*, proposed for the *common* advantage of the Christian world, and not of his particular church. I mean the *Second* volume of DR. GEDDES's *Translation of the Bible*. I really
would

The subjects of this poem have been from necessity various and numerous, far beyond my original conception.

N O T E.

would not *trust* myself to *criticise* the Translation itself, after I had read the fifth Chapter of Judges v. 30. where for the words, " To every man a damsel or two," Dr. Geddes *translates*, by way of a *spirited* and *inviting* improvement, " *a Girl*, A COUPLE OF GIRLS, *to each* brave *man !*" I will have nothing to do with THE DOCTOR's *Bravery*; but I intend to make a few observations on the *Preface* alone, which is very extraordinary indeed, and by no means in the spirit which the sacred writings seem to recommend. I am always pleased with every serious attempt to elucidate the Scriptures, and am as ready as any man to acknowledge the merit and learning of an industrious and ingenious scholar. But though I differ essentially from Dr. Geddes, I am sure I shall never call him " apostate, infidel, or heretic" in general terms, as *he knows* some persons will do; (Pref. p. 4.) but I may oppose an opinion to an opinion. . The cause in which he is engaged is not a trifling cause, nor is it, as we are sometimes told, an object of *mere classical* criticism. I think there is an unbecoming levity in the Doctor's manner more frequently than I could wish, and he expresses his sentiments in language not easily understood at all times, nor according to the genius and common grammar of the English tongue. But his meaning and opinion is, that " the " *Historical* Books of the Old Testament were *not divinely in-* " *spired*." He tells us (p. 12.) of a partial and *putative* in- " spiration," and that the writers had not " a perpetual and " *unerring sufflation*." I do not quite understand the terms, as they are *too sublime* for a plain Englishman, but I *suppose* they are very fine, and I *suppose* their meaning from other sentences in the preface. He says (p. 3.) that " The He- " brew Historians wrote them from *such human documents* " as they could find, *popular traditions, old songs, and public* " *registers*." Singular materials truly for divine inspiration ! But he says also, " I venture (and it is indeed venturing a " great deal) I *venture* to lay it down *as a certain truth*, that " there is *no intrinsic evidence* of the Jewish Historians *being* " *divinely inspired; that there is nothing* in the style or arrange- " ment in the whole colour or complexion of their compo- " sitions that speaks the guidance of an unerring spirit, but " that *on the contrary*, every thing *proclaims* the fallible and " failing writer." (p. 5.) Dr. G. declares also, " After " reading the Hebrew writings, and finding *to his full convic-* " *tion* so many intrinsic marks of fallibility, error and in-
consistency,

tion. But a mighty and majestic river in it's course
through a diversity of countries not only winds and
murmurs through the vallies, but contends and foams
among rocks, and precipices, and the confluence of tor-
rents. Still it's tendency is to the ocean, to which it
pays it's last tribute and is finally lost in that immen-
sity. In literature the mind resembles such a course.
All it's exertions may be turned into one grand and general

NOTE.

" .consistency, not to say *downright absurdity*," (p. 11.) he
could not believe their inspiration, even if he were taught
it by an angel. I have thus introduced the reader to the
Doctor's most explicit opinion, but I will present him with
his solemn affirmation, and he will easily decide on the propriety, the reasoning and the consistency of it. " *I value them
not the less,* (says Dr. Geddes) " *because* I deem them *not divinely
" inspired.*" (p. 12.) If a man can seriously assert, that *the
Scriptures inspired by* God (upon that supposition being granted) are *not more valuable* than the productions of a mere fallible wretched *creature like man* in his best estate, I really
could not lose my time in argument with that man however
learned or however gifted. He has degraded himself from
that rank of literature and of sound understanding, which
gives him a title to be answered. Dr. Geddes, as a scholar,
should *re*-consider his character, and as a professed Christian, he should *re*-examine his principles. I cannot discuss
the doctrine of inspiration in this place; it cannot be expected that I should. But the tendency of *all* the proceedings of our scholars and guides in literature, and in the state,
and in religion, should be carefully watched. The open
blasphemy and low scurrility of Thomas Paine has been
set aside by just argument, and the law of the land has
armed itself against it's effect in society.§ Mr. LEWIS *Member of Parliament,* has attacked *the Bible* in another and in a
shorter

NOTE ON THE NOTE.

§ I am glad to bear testimony to the excellence of Mr.
Erskine's eloquent *declamation* in the Court of K. B. in
that cause, on Newton, Boyle, Locke, and other great men,
the defenders of Christianity.—But my *general* opinion of
Mr. Erskine's talent for writing and public speaking is very
different. (See a future note on this Poem, Part 4.)

neral direction. The mind, if well regulated, remem-
bers from whence it came, and feels that all it's powers
and

shorter manner †, *blasphemous as far as it goes*, and tending
to discredit and traduce it's authority. And last Dr. GED-
DES, a Translator of the Bible, versed in the original language and in Hebrew criticism, has *now begun* his attack
also on the *historical* parts, which, if they are not part of
the *inspired* writings, are not intitled to the name of sacred
Scriptures. It is difficult to say, where these attacks will
end. The times are so precarious, and revolt from all authority human and divine so frequent, that the magistrate,
the satirist, and the critic have an united office. *If* the *historical* parts of the Bible are given up, another man will arise
and object to the *poetical* parts. These will be allowed to
have sublimity, and dignity; but *why* should they be considered as *inspired*. All poetry, we shall be told, is in some
sense inspired; Homer and Æschylus and Shakespeare, and
why not the Hebrew bards. The *moral* portion of the Scriptures is evidently full of wisdom and sound sense, and I suppose we shall soon hear it may be *the work of a philosopher*,
and that morality is not matter of inspiration. A fourth writer may first insinuate *with great respect* and then prove that all
prophecy is ambiguous, and that the prophecies in the Bible
may be conjectural, and therefore no reliance can be had
on *their* inspiration. Lastly we may be told, that the *doctrinal*
parts are so much above as well as contrary ‡ to *human* reason,

NOTE ON THE NOTE.

† In "The Monk, a Romance." See above. Pref. p. ii. and
iii. of Part 4.
‡ As the subject is so important and words are so frequently
misapplied or misapprehended, it is always of use to remember the words *Faith and Reason* as contradistinguished to each
other. Mr. Locke has defined them with a clearness and a
precision which never can be exceeded, and which never
should be forgotten in thought or in conversation. "REA-
"SON, as contradistinguished to *Faith*, I take to be the dis-
"covery of the certainty or probability of such proposi-
"tions or truths, which the mind arrives at by deduction
"made from such ideas which it has got by the use of it's
"natural faculties, namely, by sensation or reflection.—
"FAITH, on the other side, is the assent to any proposition
"not thus made out *by the deductions of reason*, but upon the
"credit of the proposer, as coming from GOD, in some ex-
"traordinary way of communication. This way of dis-
"covering truths to men, we call *Revelation*." Locke's
Essay on the H. U. B. 4. C. 18.

and faculties are but ministerial. I think it is some-
where expressed in the concise sublimity of Plato, Προς
το

NOTE.

son, that they could not come *from God.* Thus might the
whole fabric vanish into air, *into thin air :* or to reverse
Mr. Gibbon's phrase, thus might "the triumphant banner
"of the heathen Capitol be *again* erected on the ruins of the
"Church of Christ." Still we are to sit silent, still we are to
hear with patience the outrageous presumption of man before
his merciful Creator! while "The world and it's adora-
"ble AUTHOR, *his* attributes and essence, *his* power and
"rights and *duty* (I tremble to pronounce the word) be all
"*brought together to be judged—*BEFORE US."§ We are to as-
ble *in the Temple* with all our princes, and lords, and poten-
tates, and venerable orders, and our high officers in all
the gradations and dignities of our state and hierar-
chy, till some CHAMPION of anarchy and infidelity be
brought forth, as in sport, and placed *between the pillars.* He
may "bow himself with all his might," but his strength,
I trust, will not be from above; he will "*feel* (the nature of)
the pillars whereupon the house standeth!" I speak this *in general.*
I do not apply it to Dr. Geddes or any such scholar. It is
not now for the first time that *the Canon, and the inspiration,
and the authenticity of the Scriptures* have been examined ; and
their

NOTE ON THE NOTE.

§ Ogden's Sermons, Hallifax's edit. vol. 1. p. 2.—There
was something peculiarly amiable in the kind and disinterested office which the late Bishop of St. Asaph, Dr. HALLIFAX
undertook in the vindication of the memory and writings of
two great men, *(quales et quantos viros!)* Bishop Butler and
Dr. Ogden. It will be an eternal honour to that very acute,
learned, and most judicious prelate. Cicero shall speak for
this prelate; as no man better understood the strength and
application of his language. "Idoneus meâ quidem senten-
"tia, præsertim quum et IPSE *Eum audiverit* et *scribat de mor-
"tuo;* ex quo nulla suspicio est amicitiæ causâ eum esse men-
"titum." Cic. de Clar. Orat. Sect. 15. What such a
writer as Dr. Hallifax has told, who would tell again? I only
speak in honour to the memory of a Scholar, whose name
should be *recorded.* Το γαρ γερας εστι θανοντων.

το αἴδιον ἐδλεπεν. Under the influence and persuasion of this great and master principle the mind so prepared, whether serious, or gay, or thoughtful, or sprightly, or even fantastic in it's humour, is still performing it's proper office. Philosophy and criticism cannot reach some subjects, which sap the foundation and support of well-being. Playfulness, ridicule, wit, and humour, are the auxiliaries and light-armed forces of truth, and their power, in detachments, is equally felt with the main strength of the body.

There is one description and sect of men, to whom more than common reprehension is due, and who cannot be held up too frequently to the public scorn and abhorrence. I mean the modern philosophers of the French system. Mr. Burke has thundered upon them, and his lightning shone through their darkest recesses. "*The sudden blaze far round illumined Hell.*" This monstrous compound of the vanity and weakness of

---

NOTE.

their internal evidence has often taught a different lesson. I cannot help offering one suggestion, as it is new to me. If there is a subject in the Bible which has been particularly *singled out for profane ridicule*, it is that of Jonah being swallowed up in the whale's belly three days and three nights. Yet, as if to confound human wisdom, or sagacity, or vanity, and as an eternal lesson to human presumption on the fitness and unfitness of *the subjects* of inspiration, THE SAVIOUR OF THE WORLD HIMSELF thought proper to choose and to appropriate this event TO HIMSELF. "*As* Jonah was three days and three nights in the whale's belly, so *shall* THE SON OF MAN *be three days and three nights in the heart of the earth!*" St. Matt. c. 12. v. 40.—I solemnly protest I have no other object in view in whatever I have written, but the good of man in all his best interests, *complicated* as they are at *this* awful and *pressing* hour. More is *yet* in our power than we may even imagine; but *all* the orders of the state must unite vigorously and powerfully in their *specific* functions to preserve it. The priests and ministers of the Lord must also stand between the porch and the altar, and exert themselves " before their eyes begin to wax dim that they may not see, " and ere *the lamp of* God *goeth out in the temple of the Lord,* " WHERE THE ARK OF GOD WAS!"†

† Sam. b. 1. ch. 3. v. 3.

of the intellect, and the fury of the passions in some of
them, this " facinus majoris abollæ," should be exposed
with the full strength of: argument and of reason, and
with occasional ridicule, to the English nation in every
point of view. In other philosophers of this system, there is a calmness and composure in their
mental operations more savage than the violence
of the former. Their subject is *the living
man*. Before them he is delivered bound hand and
foot. On him their experiments are to be tried; and
when his whole composition, moral and political, is
either racked, or disjointed, or the minuter parts of it
laid bare to the eye and the very circulation of the
fluids, as it were, shewn in the agonizing subject ; this
they savagely call, studying and improving human nature
by the new light. But I will not proceed on this subject.
Great and venerable is the name and influence of the
true philosophy. The word may be disgraced for a
season, but *the love of wisdom* must always command
refpect. When we compare these modern philosophers who *reject* all revelation, with the philosophers
of antiquity, and in particular those of the Stoic sect,
who *were ignorant* of it, the difference, to say no more,
is indeed striking. What were Socrates, and Plato,
and Epictetus, and Antoninus ! Before such lights,
shining in the darkness and gloom of the heathen fir-
mament;

> Conditur omne
> Stellarum vulgus, *fugiunt sine nomine signa.* (d)

As I am speaking of Philosophy, I may be excufed
if I say a few words of that language, in which it's
power has been most conspicuous. I see no more pe-
dantry in the knowledge and study of *the Greek* tongue,
than of the French or the German. But when I consider that every subject in philosophy, in history; in
oratory, and in poetry, whatever can dignify or em-
bellish human society in it's most cultivated state, has
there found the highest authors ; that the principles of
composition are better taught and more fully exemplified
than in any other language ; that the Greek writers are

PART IV.   e   the

(d) Manil. Astron. L. 1. v. 470.

the universal legislators in taste, criticism, and just composition, from whom there is no appeal, and who will be found unerring directors; I would with peculiar emphasis and earnestness request young men of fortune, ability, and polished education, not to cast off the study of the Greek writers, when they leave the university. A few hours devoted to this study in every week will preserve and improve their knowledge. It will animate the whole mass of their learning, will give colour to their thoughts and precision to their expressions. There is no necessity either to quote or to speak Greek; but the constant perusal of the historians, philosophers, orators, and poets will be felt and perceived. In parliament and at the bar it would be most conspicuous.(a) They who are wise will secretly attend to this recommendation, which must be disinterested, and proceeds from long experience.

In regard to the manner and the plan of *this* Poem on the P. of L. I have something to say, but my respect to the reader prevents me from saying much. It aspires not to the manner or the praise of THE DUN-CIAD, or to any thing whatsoever in common with that great performance. The *original motive* of it however, in my opinion, is as far superior in importance and dignity, as the power and ability of the author fall short of that poetical excellence, which none hereafter must hope to rival or perhaps to attain. It's general subject is

---

NOTE.

(a) Plutarch describes the first Marcellus, (the first of that distinguished race) as a warrior of experience and intrepidity, humane and polished in his manners and a great lover of the Greek literature; the words are these: Τη μεν εμπειρια πολεμικος, τη φυσει φιλοπολεμος· τω δε αλλω τροπω σωφρων, φιλανθρωπος, Ελληνικης παιδειας και λογων, αχρι τε τιμαν και θαυμαζειν τες κατορθυντας, εραστης. Plut. Vit. Marcell. p. 242. vol. 2. Ed. Bryan.—As we have now *so many gentlemen of fortune and family and education and ability* among the officers of the army and the militia, I wish they may read this note, and employ some of their vacant hours in valuable studies and, like the great chiefs among the ancients, resume and vindicate the honour of learned military leisure.

isLITERATURE however exerted, whether for the benefit or for the injury of mankind. It has nothing of the
mock epic. It is a dialogue; has something of a dramatic cast, and is an excursus. The subjects follow
each other; and if I am not mistaken, they are neither
confounded nor confused. If there be in the whole
composition any passage, any sentence, or any expression, which, according to the specific nature of the subject, can justly offend even female delicacy; which, from
the manner of it, a gentleman would refuse to write, or
a man of virtue to admit into his thoughts; which violates the high, and discriminating, and honourable, and
directing principles of human conduct, it is to me matter of serious and of solemn regret. *Naturæ imperio
gemimus.* I am not conscious of having admitted any
such passage, or sentence, or expression. I have never
yet heard *such* an objection to my work. If it can be
pointed out, I will erase it with much concern and
with greater indignation.

I should also give a few words to *the manner* of the
notes which I have annexed, and which are so frequent
and so copious. I wished not, as Boileau expresses it,
to prepare tortures for any future Salmasius, (*f*) and I too
well know my own insignificance to expect any comment on my writings but from my own pen. I have
made no allusion which I did not mean to explain. But
I had something further in my intention. The notes are
not always merely explanatory; they are (if I have
been able to execute my intention) of a structure rather
peculiar to themselves. Many of them are of a nature
between an essay and an explanatory comment. There
is much matter in a little compass, suited *to the exi-
gency* of the times. As they take no particular
form of composition, they are not matter of criticism
in that particular respect. I expatiated on the casual
subject which presented itself; and when ancient or
modern writers expressed the thoughts better than I
could

e 2

(*f*) " *Aux Saumaises futurs préparer des tortures.*"
Boil. Sat. 9. v. 64.

could myself, I have given the original languages. No man has a greater contempt for *the parade* of quotation (as such) than I have. My defign is not to quote words, but to enforce right fentiments in the manner which I think beft adapted to the purpose, after much reflection. To most of my readers those languages are familiar; and if any person, not particularly conversant in them, should honour the notes with a perusal, I think the force of the observations may be felt without attending to the Greek or Latin. In all regular compositions I particularly dislike *a mixture of languages.* It is uncouth or inelegant, and sometimes marks a want of power in the writer. In works of any dignity or consequence, it is adviseable, if a passage from any ancient author is quoted, to translate that passage in the text, and put the original at the bottom of the page, if necessary. We have in this respect the authority and example of Cicero, Bishop Hurd, and Sir William Jones.

In general, I could say all I wished in the text and comment. Some subjects are indeed so important, that they should be held forth to public light and viewed in every point. SATIRE, in this respect, has peculiar force. Vice is not unfrequently repressed, and folly and presumptuous ignorance and conceit sometimes yield or vanish at the first attack, and like the fabled spirits before the spell of the enchanter,

> *Primâ vel voce* Canentis
> *Concedunt,* CARMENQUE TIMENT AUDIRE SECUN-
> DUM.(g)

I again declare to the public, that *neither my name, nor my situation in life will ever be revealed.* I pretend not to be " the sole depositary of my own secret;" but where it is confided, there it will be preserved and locked up *for ever.* I have an honourable confidence in the human character, when properly educated and rightly instructed. My secret will for ever be preserved, *I know*, under every change of fortune or

of

(g) Lucan, L. 6. v. 527.

of political tenets; while honour, and virtue, and religion, and friendly affection, and erudition, and the principles of a gentleman, have binding force and authority upon minds so cultivated and so dignified..

My Poem *and all and each of the notes to it* were written *without any co-operation* whatsoever. I expect *the fullest assent and credit* to this my solemn assertion. I expect it, *because I speak the truth.* I have *not* been assisted by Doctors in any faculty. If indeed I had written to please a particular man, a minister, a chief in opposition, a party, any set, or any description of men *exclusively,* literary or political, there is not a man of understanding in the country who does not perceive that I should, or rather that I *must* have written in another style, thought and argument. Of such motives I profess myself nor skilled nor studious. My appeal is *direct* to my Country. I know and feel the situation in which at this moment SHE stands. There is now no balance *left* in Europe. All is preparing to sink under ONE DESOLATING TYRANNY. My opinion however is, that by the mercy of Providence, and by the unremitted attention and labours of our *constitutional* statesmen, and the *united* efforts of all that are loyal, brave, opulent, powerful, or dignified, WE may yet " be able to stand IN THIS EVIL DAY, *and having done all* TO STAND." Let us stand therefore, as the chosen nation of old, the insulated memorial of true Religion; and the ONLY Asylum of balanced Liberty. I profess myself convinced, and therefore have I written. I entered into the sanctuary of the Hebrews and heard the voice of their prophet: " Credidi, propter quod locutus sum." This was the voice which I heard, and it was a voice, as Milton would express it, " thundering out of Sion." Under this persuasion and conviction, I will say of this work, there is in it but one hand and one intention. It will be *idle* to conjecture concerning the author, and *more than foolish* to be *very* inquisitive. To my adversaries I have nothing to reply. I never will reply. I could with the most perfect charity sing a requiem over their deceased criticisms, if I were master of what Statius calls the "Exequiale

quiale sacrum, carmenque *minoribus umbris* utile.*(h)* Those whom I wished to please, I have pleased. If I have diffused any light, it is from *a single orb;* whether temperate in the horizon or blazing in the meridian. My aspect is not in conjunction: if I culminate at all, it is from the Equator.

Thus much to silly curiosity and frivolous garrulity. But to persons of higher minds and of more exalted and more generous principles, who have the spirit to understand, and the patience to consider, the nature and the labour of my work, I would address myself in other language and with other arguments. I would declare *to them,* that when I consider the variety and importance and extent of the subjects, I might say that it was written, " though for no other cause yet for this, that pos- " terity may know, that we have not loosely through " silence permitted things to pass away as in a dream." I would declare also *to them,* that I deliver it *as* A LI-TERARY MANIFESTO *to this Kingdom* in a season un-propitious to learning or to poetry, in a day of darkness and of thick gloominess, and in an hour of turbulence, of terror, and of uncertainty. Such persons will be satisfied, if the great cause of mankind, of regulated society, of religion, of government, and of good man-ners, is *attempted* to be maintained with strength and with the application of learning. To them it is a matter of very little or rather of no moment at all, by whom it is effected. They have scarce a transitory question to make on the subject. To such understandings I wil-lingly submit my composition, and to them I dedicate the work.

I shall only add, that *if* they should read *all* the Parts of this Poem on the Pursuits of Literature with candour and with attention, whatever the connection between them or the method may be, they will most assuredly find, " *that uniformity of thought and design,* which will " *always* be found in the writings of *the same* person, " WHEN HE WRITES WITH SIMPLICITY AND IN " EARNEST."

(*h*) Stat. Theb. L. 6. v. 123.

THE

PURSUITS OF LITERATURE:

A SATIRICAL POEM.

PART IV.

AUTHOR.

OH, for that sabbath's dawn ere Britain wept,
And France before THE CROSS believ'd and slept!
(Rest to the state, and slumber to the soul!)
Ere yet the brooding storm was heard to roll
In fancy's ear o'er many an Alpine rock,   5
Or Europe trembled at the fated shock;
Ere by his lake GENEVA'S ANGEL stood,
And wav'd his scroll prophetic (a) o'er the flood,

         With

 (a) It is remarkable that *in Switzerland* appeared THE THREE PERSONS, whose principles, doctrines, and practice, (*as it seems to me*) have primarily and ultimately effected the great change and downfal of regal and of lawful power in Europe. Calvin, in religion; Rousseau, in politics; and Neckar by his administration.

With names (as yet unheard) and symbols drear,
'Calvin in front, and Neckar in the rear,   10

                                        But

tration. Calvin and his disciples were never friends to monarchy and episcopacy. I shall not *here* contend politically or the-
ologically with Bishop Horsley concerning Calvin. Indeed I
never yet stood gaping on that *copper* oracle. A Poet's words
are better for a poet. I have looked into history and, as I think,
have found them true. Dryden speaks of Calvin thus, and re-
markably enough;

    The *last* of all the litter scap'd by chance,
    " *And from Geneva first infested* FRANCE."

                         (Hind and Panther. B. 1. v. 172.)
ROUSSEAU, (I speak of him *only* as a political writer) by the unjus-
tifiable, arbitrary, and cruel proceedings against him, his writings
and his person, in France, (where he was a stranger and to whose
tribunals he was not amenable) was stimulated to pursue his
researches into the origin and expedience of *such* government,
and of *such* oppression, which, otherwise, he probably, never
would have discussed; till he reasoned himself into the desperate
doctrine of political equality, and gave to the world his fatal
present, " *The Social Contract.*" Of *this* work the French, since
the Revolution, have never once lost sight. With them it is first
and last, and midst, and without end in all their thoughts and
public actions. Rousseau, is, I believe, the only man to whom
they have paid an implicit and *undeviating* reverence; and, without a figure, have worshipped in the Pantheon of their new idol-
atry, like another Chemos, " the *obscene* dread of Gallia's sons."
—Different from these, came NECKAR. With intentions, as I
firmly think, upright, pure and just, but with a mind impotent
and unequal to the great work, and with principles foreign to
                                      the

But chief Equality's vain priest, Rousseau,

A sage in sorrow nurs'd, and gaunt with woe,

F

By

the nature of the government he was called to regulate, reform and conduct, "a fatal stranger" for France. He *oppressed* every subject sacred and civil with too much *verbiage*. He was sanctioned by popular prejudice, and marked by aristocratical hatred; a sort of " *Arpinas Volscorum a monte*." He came to lay open and disclose (and he did lay them open to the very bottom) the mystery and iniquity of French finance and of French treasuries. But he brought with him to the concerns of a great and tottering empire (which perhaps might have been maintained and *consolidated*) the little mind of a provincial banker, and the vanity inseparable from human nature, when elevated beyond hope or expectation. What was the consequence? for a while indeed,

Hic Cimbros et summa pericula rerum

Excipit, et soLus trepidantem *protegit* Urbem. †

But the original leaven in *his* political composition was *popular*; and that leavened the whole lump. We know the rest. His advice, first in the calling together (at all) of *the States General*, and afterwards in the formation and distribution of them, gave the devoted King to the scaffold, and the monarchy of France to irreversible dissolution.—For my own part when I contemplate the convulsions of Europe, and the fatal desolation which attends republican principles, *wherever they are introduced*, I cannot but rest with a momentary pleasure on the picture which Plato in his *imaginary* republic, (the *only* one I ever could bear) has drawn of a man fatigued with the view of public affairs and retiring from them in the hope of tranquillity: the sentiments are such as the French formerly would have called, " *Les Delasseniens de l'hommé sensible.*" The words are these:

By persecution train'd and popish zeal,

Ripe with his wrongs ,to frame the dire (b) appeal,

What time *his work* THE CITIZEN began,   15

And gave to France the social savage, Man.

    Was it for this, in Leo's fost'ring reign

Learning uprose with tempests in her train;

Was every gleam deceitful, every ray

But idle splendor from the orb of day ?   20

Say, were the victims mark'd from earliest time,

The Flamens conscious of a nation's crime ?

Why smoaked the altars with the new perfume,

If heav'n's own fire descends but to consume?

                            Alas,.

"Ταυτα παντα λογισμω λαβων,ησυχιαν εχων και τα αυτυ πρατ-
των, διον εν χειμωνι κονιορτυ και ζαλης υπο πνευματος φερομενυ
υπο τειχιον υποστας, ορων τυς αλλυς καταπιμπλαμενυς ανομιας,
αγαπᾶ ει πη αυτος καθαρος αδικιας τε και ανοσιων εργων, τον τε
ενθαδε βιον βιωσεται, και την απαλλαγην αυτυ μετα καλης ελπιδος
ιλεως τε και ευμενης απαλλαξεται.

      Plato de Repub. L. 6. p. 496, Op. vol. 2. Ed. Serrani.

    (b) " Le Contrat Social, par J. J. Rousseau, CITOYEN de Geneve.

Alas, proud Gallia's fabric to the ground   25

What arm shall level, or what might confound!

Oh for that hand, which o'er the walls of Troy (c)

His lightning brandish'd with a furious joy,

F 2   Her

(c) It certainly would be *convenient*, (if we can for a moment
trifle with such a subject as the present French war) to march
to *Paris*, " *and, like another* (Bryant) *fire another Troy.*" We
have little hope, but from such assistance.—See " a Dissertation
concerning the War of Troy, and the Expedition
of the Grecians, as described by Homer; shewing, that no
such expedition was undertaken, and that no such city
of Phrygia existed." Published in 1796, but there is no date
to the title page. I find it difficult to give an opinion on this
ingenious treatise. Whatever comes from the author of " The
Analysis of ancient Mythology" should be treated with very
great respect. His character is * venerable, and his erudition,
as I think, without an equal. Of all subjects, I should have
thought this subject was one, on which an enquiry might have
been instituted without offence. Yet this has not been the case.
The offence has been considered as deep and wide, and the influence
of the principle, in some respects, dangerous and alarming.
The faith of history has been represented as attacked
in its strongest fortress, and even the sacred writings, as matter of
historical faith, implicated in the discussion. Some persons
have even declared that Mr. Bryant had no right to touch the
subject. That nothing can be more contrary to reason than
to suppose that the existence of a city, and a war, of which we
have read with delight from our boyish days, should be called

in

* Pursuits of L. Part II. v. 189.

Her state, her arms, her fleets, her very name

Gave, as in mock'ry, to poetic fame,   30

                                 And

in question. That their pleasure is snatched from them: and such a poem, without an historical fact for a basis, cannot be interesting. They allow the amplification of poetry, and it's embellishments, and even the anachronisms of Homer. But Troy did exist, and the Grecians did once besiege it, and Hector, Achilles, Agamemnon, and Diomede were as real heroes, as the Archduke Charles, Buonaparte, Lord Cornwallis or Tippoo Saib in modern wars. I really should smile at many of these objections, if they did not frequently come from persons of consequence and of learning. Most certainly however I will quarrel with no man " about Sir Archy's great Grandmother." They who are acquainted with the science and subject of *probabilities* will best decide the question for themselves, and I will not intrude my judgment. It is a question of probability and not of proof. I am equally pleased with a poem founded on the metamorphosis of Apuleius or on any modern fiction, if all the essential and integral parts of a poem are preserved: if the characters, manners and actions are human, and consistent with the supposed situations of the personages. This to me is sufficient, and perhaps poetry, as such, may be a gainer by Mr. Bryant's interpretation. I rather hail the omen in these times of poetical sterility. But nothing can be further from the dignity of Mr. B's character, than the imputation of having attacked the faith and credibility of ancient, or of any, *history*. It is scarcely entitled to notice. What was Troy? with what part of history is it connected? Is not the Trojan war an insulated solitary fact? If it were done away, is any historical event whatever made to fall with it? When it is stated that *four hundred and thirty* ships (no matter of what size) were employed by the Grecians in the Trojan war in the twelfth century, and only *eighty nine*

                                 in

And with the fire of Philip' son, unfurl'd

His classic standard o'er a wond'ring world,

Till " *Homer's sprite did tremble all for grief,*

" *And curs'd th'access of that celestial thief.*" (*d*)

Oh, for a Bryant's hand!—

O C T A-

in the Pelopopnesian war in the fifth century before Christ, is this matter of *serious* history? Is not the whole allowed to pass even the bounds of any probability, but the poet's? I remember hearing a gentleman state similar questions to these with much earnestness and apparent conviction, but without warmth. He seemed to understand something of the subject; and though I thought some points were pressed indiscreetly and unnecessarily by Mr. Bryant, I replied that I thought *nearly* as he did, and I said with the most good-natured Εποχη of the Academics, " *Almost* thou persuadest me to be a *Bryantian.*"—I think they who are the strongest in opposition to Mr. Bryant, if they were even Inquisitors§, and could force him to hold a lighted torch in his hand and make a retractation of his errors, and the *amende honorable* in the *Eglise de notre Dame de* Cybele *Mere de tous les Dieux Païens,* would be contented with the Catholic form of words: Questi erano gli scherzi d'una penna poetica, non gli sentimenti d'un animo catolico!" Yet considering all that I have heard, and *the quarter* from which it came, *Curius* quid sentit, et ambo *Scipiadæ,* and the insignificance

§ I am sure *Gilbert Wakefield* is even *more than an Inquisitor* in all his principles literary, civil, and religious. See his indecent letter to Mr. Bryant on the war of Troy. But above all, see his Letter to Mr. Wilberforce. The Secretary to the Duke of Alva under Philip II. or the Public Accuser of the Revolutionary Tribunal, under Roberspierre, never exhibited such a paper. *There is no deceit in Gilbert Wakefield:* " *He is, just what he seems.*" It is plain to see *what* he expects, and *why* he writes.

OCTAVIUS.

Methinks you smile, 35

And fain would land me on the wand'ring isle,

Where the learn'd drain *Acrasia*'s foaming bowl,

Till *round the Sun* their heads with Gebelin's (*e*) roll ;

          Nor

cance of the question itself, but as a matter of amusement; though in common with many others, I should have lost much individual gratification and instruction, yet I wish this Dissertation on the war of Troy *had never been written at all.*

(*d*) Two lines from Sir Walter Raleigh's Sonnet, prefixed to Spenser's Fairy Queen.

(*e*) *Gebelin.*—If many of the learned world have thought Mr. Bryant unadvised in the discussion of the war of Troy in the twelfth century A. C. what must we say to Mr. Court de Gebelin, who has actually endeavoured *to reason men into a belief,* that, *the Founders of the Roman State,* ROMULUS *and* REMUS, were only allegorical personages, and were in reality representatives of *the Sun* and worshipped as such. Mr. Gebelin is a man of the most various erudition, and if he were as well known as Mr. Bryant, his attempt would have been noticed. But few people perhaps have had the curiosity to look into nine volumes in 4to of the "Monde Primitif analysé et comparé avec le Monde Moderne par M. Court de Gebelin." It may be entertaining to some persons, if I give a *few* particulars of this singular question. The *Fourth* Volume of Mr. Gebelin's work consists of the " Histoire Religieux du *Calendrier,* ou des Fêtes Anciennes." The *fifth* Chapter of the *second* Book (Vol. 4.) is the " Histoire des *Gemeaux* Romains Romulus et Remus." Mr. G. says,
            " Les

Nor heed the pause of (*f*) Douglas, Wakefield's rage,

Nor Hallam (*g*) trembling for the sacred page,   40

Nor

" Les *Romains* eurent aussi leurs *Allegories* sur le *double Soleil* suc-
cessif de l'année; ils *l'appliquerent à* leur *Remus et Romulus.*
Les noms sont *allegoriques,* et tous *relatifs à l'année."* p. 264.
Remus, it seems, signified THE SUN *in the winter,* and Romulus,
in the summer ! By an *easy* proof, he says, " Ils en firent la fête
des *Lemures* pour *Remures,* &c. p. 263. In the sixth chapter
of the same Book, we read: Nous avons *vu* dans le chapitre
précédent, *que* ROMULUS *etoit* LE SOLEIL; que tout le *prouvoit:*
—And what is the proof? Truly this : " Le nom de sa mere,
celui de son pere, son frere, la mort de son frere (*Remus*), son
propre nom, &c. &c." Q. E. D.—Mr. Gebelin has not yet done,
nor is Mr. Gebelin yet satisfied. He next converts, by means
of his *solar* microscope, Romulus into *Hercules!* Hear his words.
" Ce qu'exprimoient à cet ègard les Grecs par l'Apothéose d'
Hercule, les Romains l'exprimerent par l'Apothéose de Romulus." But when he speaks of *Quirinus,* another name of Romulus, the force of art and of *proof* can go no further. La voici.
" *Quirinus* (nom de Romulus) la traduction *litérale* de *Mel-
carthe,* on *Melicerte,* que portoit *Hercule* chez les *Tyriens,* EST
UNE AUTRE PREUVE, *qu'on regardoit* ROMULUS *comme* LE SO-
LEIL." p 269 !!!!!!—I cannot help observing that in this same
4th Vol. p. 422. Mr. Gebelin informs us that, " Sur le 18 Fev-
rier on célébroit *la Fête de Romulus,* (and at the same time, rather
inauspiciously to be sure) on célébroit LA FETE DES FOUX.'' I
suppose on the celebration of LA FETE DES FOUX, cards of in-
vitation were sent round by the Pontifex Maximus to the *Antiquaries* of those days, and I really think, if Mr. Gebelin had been
produced at that time he would not have been *without his card,*

with

Nor Gillies (*h*) *crying*, what shall we peruse,

My history's now mere records of the Muse,

And trust to Buonaparte's iron pen, (*i*)

The tale of Rome shall be Troy's tale again.

AUTHOR.

---

with a few others, to be distributed *among his friends.*—Indeed these *deliramenta doctrinæ* are sometimes amusing, but in reality they are rather a subject of serious regret from their consequences on the public mind. There is no end of the absurdities from this source, when we resolve all ancient persons and events into allegories and Egyptian mysteries; till as we have just seen, ROMULUS AND REMUS, *the Founders of the Roman Empire*, become (according to Monsieur Gebelin's *Order of Firing* after a grand *Escopetterie*, or volley, *of serpents and stars*) transformed into ROMAN SUNS; Remus *in the Winter*, and Romulus *in the Summer!*—See the *proofs* above.

(*f*) The Rt. Rev. Dr. JOHN DOUGLAS, the present Bishop of Salisbury, Author of the Criterion, and of other acute pieces of reasoning, which will be long remembered and admired.

(*g*) Dr. Hallam, the present Dean of Bristol. (1797.)

(*h*) Author of *a* History of *Greece*; but I shall say no more than that Dr. Gillies's solicitude is groundless, when he fears that it will be mistaken for the work of *the Muses*.

AUTHOR.

No; other thoughts my lab'ring soul employ, 45
That springs anew to long-forgotten joy;
I range in Fancy's consecrated round,
And meet the poet on a poet's ground,
Nor seek historic truth of time and place,
But truth of manners, character, and grace.   50

The Bards, who once the wreaths of glory wore,
Cloath'd in translucent veil their wondrous lore,
The tales they sung a willing age believ'd,
Charm'd into truth, and without guile deceiv'd;
Where'er they rov'd, young Fancy and the Muse 55
Wav'd high their mirror of a thousand hues;
They gaz'd; and as in varying guise pourtray'd,
Aëreal phantoms hov'ring round them play'd,

G   Gave

(i) The tremendous conquefts of Buonaparte in Italy and in
Germany remind us too much of the words of the Roman His-
torian. " Si CAPTIVOS aspiceres, Molossi, Thessali, Macedones,
Bruttius, Apulius; si POMPAS, aurum, purpuræ, signa, tabulæ,
Tarentinæque deliciæ." Flor. Lib. 1. C. 18.
    PART IV.

Gave to each fleeting form, that shot along,

Existence everlasting as their song,   60

And as by nature's strength the tablet grew,

Rapture the pencil guided as they drew.

OCTAVIUS..

Nay, now you soar indeed; another flight,

And the wing'd courser bears you from my sight :

You're strangely mov'd.

AUTHOR.

The matter is my own;   65

I never shar'd the profits of the gown,

Nor yet, with Horace and myself at war,

For rhyme and *victuals* (*h*) left the starving Bar;

I never

(*h*) This was lately done by an ingenious Gentleman, educated at Eton school, William Boscawen Esquire, a Commis-
sioner of the *Victualling* Office, and (by an easy transition)
Translator of Horace. He refigned his gown, as a Counsellor
at law, to superintend *the public victuals,* and to *give himself up to
the charms of poetry,* and at last to present the hungry public
with

I never lov'd *Dean* DEWLAP's vacant looks,

Or purchas'd empty praise from empty books,   70

I leave at sales the undisputed reign

To *milk-white* (*hh*) GOSSET, and Lord (*i*) Spencer's

    train;

          G 2   No

with Horace's works *done into English verse*. The translation has had the usual fate of *mediocrity*, and therefore I say no more. But it is with particular pleasure that I inform the reader, that Mr. Boscawen, with the most classical humanity, considering *the general state of poor Barristers and Poets* at this unpropitious time, has an intention to propose the revival of the ancient custom of the *Sportula*, to be distributed at Lincoln's Inn Hall, and at the Victualling Office. The qualifications, as I have heard, are these:—*That* no Barrister be entitled to the *Sportula* except he can prove by affidavit or certificate from the Clerk of the Assizes, that he has not received five Briefs in his first twelve circuits; and for a Poet, that he has never disposed of twenty copies of any one poem of his own composing. It is feared, that the applications and certificates will be so numerous, that from the present increase of *Naval* and other *demands*, the kind intentions of *the amiable Victualler* will be frustrated.

  (hh) Not a bookseller of reputation in London, Payne, Edwards, White, Robson, Egerton, Faulder, &c. &c. is unacquainted with Dr. Gosset's "*milk-white* vellum books," where he wishes to make an exchange. The Reverend little Bibliopolish Doctor Gosset is President at all Booksales in the metropolis. He certainly is a scholar, and I believe the *auctioneer* always waits for *his* entrance, as the *Speaker* of the H. of C. waits for Mr. Pitt before public business begins. He is Inquisitor General of all editions from the Editio Princeps of the Florence Homer, down to the last edition of *Ignoramus*. Doctor Gosset's *priced* catalogues in *his own* hand are said to be in an *uninterrupted* series, except *one*. They are

          also

No German nonsense sways my English heart,

Unus'd at ghosts and rattling bones to start;   74

I never chose, in various nature. strong,

Logic for verse or history for song,

But at the magic of Torquato's strain,

Disarm'd and captive in Armida's chain,

To Godfrey's pomp Rinaldo still prefer,

Nor care if ranting Wakefield thinks I err.   80

To HURD, not (*hh*) Parr, my Muse submits her lays,

Pleas'd with advice, without a lust for praise,

Fond

alfo faid to be equal in ufe and value to " The curious collection,
" in regular and *undoubted* fucceffion, of *all the Tickets of the Ifling-*
" *ton Turnpike* from it's *firft* inftitution to the 20th of May inclu-
" five," recorded among *the prefents* made to the Antiquarian Society, when Sir Matthew Mite was admitted Fellow. (Foote's
Nabob Act 2.) I believe (but fee the Society's Archæologia *for
the record*) that it took place before the Reverend Mr. Brand
was † *the reading* Secretary, or the Earl of Leicefter *the eloquent*
PRESIDENT OF THE SOCIETY OF ANTIQUARIES. N. B. No
perfon is *now* obliged to make an inauguration fpeech, when he
is admitted Fellow of the Antiquarian Society. The *Prefident*
obferved in *one of his fpeeches*, that the cuftom ceafed and determined at Sir Matthew Mite's election, *as appeared by the record*,
copied by Mr. Foote and inferted in his Nabob.

(*i*) The Rt. Hon. Earl Spencer, the munificent, and I may
add, the learned collector of every valuable work in literature. I
record with pleafure his " *Palatine Apollo*," that *munus Apolline
dignum!*

† Mr. Brand often puts the Antiquarian Society in mind of the famous Epi-
taph:
  " Oh READER! if that *thou canft read*, &c. &c.

Fond to correct but never to defend,

And him, who marks her errors, deems her friend;

With patriot aim and no irreverent rage,   85

Without one stain of party on the page,

From Grecian springs her strength, her art she draws,

Firm in her trust, ennobled in her cause,

Her moral none, the verse (*ii*) some few disdain;

Yet not a note she sounds shall sound in vain,   90

While

(*bb*) See my account of Dr. Parr's style and writings. P. of L. Part III. p. 181, &c. with the notes. When the reader has considered the whole, perhaps he may be inclined to say with the comic poet of Athens,

Πτιλοντο μεγα ΚΟΜΠΟΛΑΚΥΘΟΥ πεσεν !
Aristoph. Acharn. Sub fin.

(*ii*) George Steevens, Esq. Editor of Shakspeare and some other ingenious Gentlemen, whom at present I shall not name, have affected to say, with equal discretion and wit, that *my* verses are *only a peg* to hang my notes upon. They are not quite original in the expreffion. Pindar said long before Mr. Steevens, Απο ΠΑΣΣΑΛΟΥ φορμιγγα λαμβανε. (Ol. 1.) But Mr. Steevens and Co. rather put me in mind of a story told of a sailor in the late mutiny (April 1797.) aboard the fleet, who after he had undergone rather a severe discipline, and was standing *dripping* upon the deck, looked up significantly to the yard-arm and said, " Well, my friends, I think I am now *wet* enough to *be hung up to dry*."—So much for George Steevens Esq. and his Brethren, " *Gentlemen of the Peg*."

While BRYANT in applause with BAKER (*k*) joins,

GIFFORD(*l*)approves, and STORER (*m*) loves the lines:

Though still, a stranger in the sacred clime,

Some say, I love not poetry, but rhyme.

Offspring of other times! ye visions old,   95

Legends, no more by gentle hands unroll'd,

Magnanimous deceits! where favour'd youth

Finds short repose from formidable truth!

Oh witness, if e'er silent in your praise,

I've pass'd, in vice or sloth, inglorious days,   100

                         But

(*k*) Sir George Baker, Bart. Physician to the King, a Gentleman of deep and extensive classical knowledge. His situation in life sufficiently declares his professional talents.

(*l*) William Gifford, Esq. Author of the Baviad and the Mæviad.

(*m*) ANTONY STORER, Esq. a Gentleman of fortune and fashion, talents and accomplishments. His attainments in literature are various and considerable; and few men have a nicer skill in the principles of just and legitimate composition than Mr. Storer. He has read Quintilian with effect, and has drawn his knowledge and judgment from the best writers and critics of antiquity and of modern times.

But rais'd for you my firm unalter'd voice,
Fancy my guide and solitude my choice.

Though now no Syren voice be heard, no strain
Ascend from Pindus (*n*) or Arcadia's plain ;   104
No Graces round th' Olympian throne of Jove
Bid the nine Virgins raise the chant of love :
The harp of Taliessin (*o*) lies unstrung,
Close by the loom round which Death's sisters sung,
Unfelt each charm of Odin's magic tree,
With many an uncouth Runic (*p*) phantasy : 110
Though

(*n*) I mean by these and several following lines to observe, that the *Pagan Fable* is now exhausted, and the specious miracles of *Gothic Romance* have never of late years produced a poet. Perhaps the latter were more adapted to true poetry than the pagan inventions. Witness the sublimer productions of modern Italy.

(*o*) A year or two ago proposals were offered by Mr. Owen to publish the works of the Bard *Taliessin*, but no encouragement could be obtained. Such is the time.

(*p*) Mr. Mathias, (the author of the Essay on the Evidence, &c. on the long-disputed subject of the poems ascribed to Rowley in the 15th century, and which I mentioned in a note to the First Part of the P. of L.) several years ago attempted to
excite

Though now no temper'd lance, no magic brand,

No Durindana (q) waves o'er fabled land;

No nightly-rounding Ariel floats unseen,

Or *flumes amazement* o'er the desert green;

No wizards hold, some blasted pine beneath,   115

Their horrid sabbath on the darken'd heath;

Say, are the days of blest delusion fled?

Must fiction rear no more her languid head?

No more the Muse her long-lost transports know,

Nor trace the fount whence living waters flow?   120

Awake, ye slumb'ring Rulers of the song!

Each in your solemn orders pass along,

In sacred radiance oe'r your mountain old

Yet once again your dignities unfold,

And fill the space; your scepter'd glories claim, 125

And vindicate the great Pierian name.

OCTA-

excite the curiosity of the public to the remains of northern antiquity, by a lyrical imitation of some Runic fragments. I wish
the example had been followed.

(q) The name of the sword of. Orlando in Ariosto,

OCTAVIUS.

Are these a poet's only themes? I fear,
No verse like this will find a patient ear.

AUTHOR.

Hear yet awhile :—the dread resistless pow'r
That works deep-felt at inspiration's hour,   130
He claims alone—

OCTAVIUS.

Who claims?

AUTHOR.

The favour'd BARD, (r)
Who nobly conscious of his juſt reward,

H   With

(r) I mean here to give a character of the Poet, *as such*, and of the sources whence the art itself is drawn. I would wish to express *generally*, what Proclus (in one of his dissertations on the Πολιτεια of Plato, Ed. fol. Basil. 1534. p. 430.) would call with a sublime dignity the Πᾶσαν Ποιητικης ἐξιν διαλάμπουσαν,"

PART IV.   when

With loftier soul and undecaying might
Paints what he feels in characters of light,   134
Hears in each blast some consecrated rhyme,
Trac'd by the spirit of the troublous clime. •
He turns : and instantaneous all around
Cliffs whiten, waters murmur, voices sound,
Portentous forms in heav'ns aërial hall
Appear, as at some great supernal call.   140
Thence oft in thought his steps ideal (*s*) haste
To rocks and groves, the wilderness or waste ;
To where old Tadmor's (*t*) regal ruins lie
In desolation's sullen majesty ;   144

Or

when the poet exerts his highest faculties, or (in the language of
Proclus in the same place) Ὁταν ενθυσιαζων, και ταις Μυσαις
κατοχος ων, κατα ΤΗΝ ΠΡΩΤΗΝ ενεργει ΚΑΙ ΕΝΘΕ-
ΟΝ ΠΟΙΗΤΙΚΗΝ."

(*s*) I speak of the effect of *local* situation on the mind of the
poet. But if he is deprived of the power of visiting these great
and awful scenes of nature, (sometimes assisted and improved
by art,) an imagination, bold and fervid, may *in some degree* supply that want by recourse to the most finished representations
of them by the more sublime painters and artists. Stuart, Wood,
and Piranesi may raise ideas worthy of the Poet, and pour upon
his fancy all the ancient dignity of Athens, of Palmyra, or of
Rome,—I cannot but present my reader with the form of *an*
Oath

Or where Carthusian (*v*) tow'rs the pilgrim draw,

And bow the soul with unresisted awe,

Where Bruno, from the mountain's pine-clad brow,

Survey'd the world's inglorious toil below;

Then, as down ragged cliffs the torrent roar'd,

Prostrate great Nature's present GOD ador'd, 150

And bade, in solitude's extremest bourn,

Religion hallow the severe sojourn,

To HIM the Painter gives his pencil's might;

No gloom too dreadful and no blaze too bright,

What time to mortal ken he dares unveil 155

THE inexpressive FORM (*x*) in semblance frail,

H 2 To

Oath on such a subject from *the last classical Poet* under the expiring monarchy of France, the famous Delisle. I am as ready on this subject, as himself, to swear at *the high altar of the Muses :*
"Helàs ! *je n'ai point vû* ce séjour enchanté,
Ces beaux lieux ou Virgile a tant de fois chanté ;
Mais j'en JURE et Virgile et ses accords sublimes,
J'irai : de l'Apennin je franchirai les cimes,
J'irai, plein de son nom, plein de ses vers sacrés,
Les lire aux mêmes lieux qui les ont inspirés.
Les Jardins L: 1.

(*t*) He built *Tadmor* in the Wilderness." Chron. B. 2. ch. 8. v. 4. It is remarkable that Mr. Wood observes, that the natives, at this day, call *Palmyra* by the original appellation of *Tadmor.*

(*v*) The famous monastery, called "The Grande Chartreuse." The retirement of Saint Bruno.

(*x*) The Pictures of the Supreme Being by Raphael and Michael Angelo. There is one picture of THE SUPREME BEING separating the light from the darkness, in the Vault of the Capella Sestina in Rome, by Michael Angelo which, I believe,
has

To the strain'd view presents the yawning tomb,
Substantial horrors and eternal doom.

To Him the pow'rs of harmony (*y*) resort,
And as with random glance and fiercer port   160
He scans th' ethereal wilderness around,
Pour on his ear the thrilling stream of sound,
Strains that from full-strung chords at distance swell,
Notes breathing soft from music's inmost cell, 164
While to their numerous pause, or accent deep,
His choral passions dread accordance keep.

Thence musing, lo he bends his weary eyes
On life and all it's sad realities;
Marks how the prospect darkens in the rear,   169
Shade blends with shade, and fear succeeds to fear,
Mid forms that flit through the malignant gloom,
Till Death unbar the cold sepulchral room.

Such is the Poet : bold, without confine,
Imagination's " *charter'd libertine*," (*z*)

He

has never been engraved. Mr. Fuseli, I think, said so when I
enquired about it. I allude also to the picture of the Last Judgment, by the fame Master.

(*y*) The power of Music on the mind of the Poet.

(*z*) " The air, *a chartered libertine*, is still."

                         Shakspere. H. V.

He scorns in apathy to float or dream   175
On listless Satisfaction's torpid stream,
But dares ALONE in vent'rous bark to ride
Down turbulent Delight's tempestuous tide;
While thoughts encount'ring thoughts in conflict fierce
Tumultuous rush, and labour into verse,   180
Then, as the swelling numbers round him roll,
Stamps on th' immortal page the visions of his soul.

OCTAVIUS.

Nay, if you feed on this cælestial strain,
You may with Gods hold converse, not with men;
Sooner the people's right shall Horsley (a) prove;
Or Sutton (aa) cease to claim the public love, 186
And e'er forego, from dignity of place,
His polish'd mind and reconciling grace;

Sooner

(a) I allude to Bishop Horsley's intemperate and unadvised speeches in Parliament. An injudicious friend is worse than an enemy. I believe Mr. Pitt thinks so.

(aa) Dr. CHARLES MANNERS SUTTON, Bishop of Norwich. A Prelate whose amiable demeanour, useful learning, and conciliating habits of life particularly recommend his episcopal character. No man appears to me so peculiarly marked out for THE HIGHEST DIGNITY of the church, *sede vacante*, as Dr. SUTTON.

Sooner Stentorian (*aaa*) Davies *cease* to talk,

And for *his* Eton leave his Bond ſtreet walk ;   190

                                         Or

(*aaa*) The Rev. Jonathan Davies D.D. Provoſt of Eton College; a learned, pleaſant, generous, open-hearted, good-tempered man, but rather too much of a Stentor in conversation :

Στεντορι εισαμενος μεγαλητορι χαλκεοφωνω,
Οσ τοσον αυδησασκ '΄ΟΣΟΝ ΑΛΛΟΙ ΠΕΝΤΗΚΟΝΤΑ.
                                         Hom. Il. 5.

MR. PROVOST has an invincible *partiality* for *the charms* of London, whenever *his duty* does not oblige him to be at his Lodge. The reaſon is ſimple. The air at Eton bites ſhrewdly, in London it ſmells wooingly, &c. &c. &c.

Extraſt from a M.S. found in *Long Chamber* at Eton, the hand writing conjeſtured to be by Dr. HEATH the Head Maſter, and *one* of the Aſſiſtants. It was found on one of MRS. HEATH's *Ball-Nights during Lent*, given to the *Lautorum Pueri* for the advantage and credit of the School. ——N. B. ETON SCHOOL; like many other great and useful public ſchools, stands in need of many *new* and *strong* regulations, which the interest of this kingdom and the nature of the times call for with a voice not to be disregarded by the masters and governors. It is not to be diſſembled, (it is MY office to speak openly and boldly) that *Boys* now actually divide themselves *into political parties.* There is indeed a general licentiousness of ſpirit among modern boys, which the public good requires to be repreſſed. It is not by a false and specious *liberality* that this evil is to be ſubdued. If masters and governors are firm and inflexible in their regulations, what can *the children* do ? I laugh at the idle appiehenſion of *rebellion* in a School. If I were the Maſter of Eton, I would begin by THE ABOLITION OF THE MONTEM immediately. It is very improper, and very foolish. There is *a meanneſs* and sometimes *an audacity* in this authorised mode of *collecting money on the highway* which I wonder *young Gentlemen* of birth and family are not *aſhamed of*, and can *even wiſh* to continue. It is something between *alms and plunder.* Harrow school has no longer it's ancient and dangerous custom of " ſhooting for the silver arrow."—I mention *the abolition of* THE MONTEM (though it occuis but once in three years) only as an introduction to *many other* salutary and necessary restrictions in ALL public Schools. I have seen the nature of a *rebellion* (as it is called) in a college and a school, and nothing can be more fooliſh and impotent. If the Parents, Friends, and Guardians co-operate with Masters of Schools and Colleges, what can *children* and young men *ultimately effect*, when it is considered, by what laws and hopes their future interest and advancement in life are bound-in, cabined, and confined ? The majority of such *petty*
                                         Revolu-

Or Warren (*b*) in his well-curv'd palm confound

An ancient guinea with a modern (*bb*) pound ;

Sooner *one* Prelate hate th' unequal glass,

And *round* (*d*) his table let the Claret pass ;

O'er

Revolutionists and embryo Democrats are always restrained *in a short time*, and their successors never feel the absence of what they never expected. Let every Master of a College and a public School boldly and vigorously and instantly adopt the words and spirit of Cicero to his friend Atticus. "*In qua* Ego *nactus*, ut mihi videbar, LOCUM RESECANDÆ LIBIDINIS ET COERCENDÆ JUVENTUTIS, vehemens fui et omne: profudi vires animi atque ingenii mei, non odio adductus alicujus *sed spe reipublicæ corrigendæ et sanandæ civitatis.* AFFLICTA EST RESPUBLICA !" —Cic. Ep. ad Attic. L. 1. E. 18. I hope this note will be regarded *with the attention it deserves from the public.*

(*b*) A learned and able Physician of the time. "*The well curved palm*" is the attitude of a modern physician, when he is about to leave his patient, and which he as naturally closes upon his fee as a lobster does his claw. As I have a high respect for the Medical art, I will gratify Dr. Warren and many other ingenious gentlemen of the profession with an Extract from one of the Elogia written by Sammarthanus; it relates to a physician whom he names *Marescottus.* " Recorderis Marescottum " nostrum *tria* se sacræ arti nostræ (Medicæ scilicet) debere profes- " sum, quibus caruisset si *propositum a parentibus sacerdotium* susce- " pisset; scilicet, sanitatem athleticam ætatis anno 82mo, *centum* " *aureorum millia,* atque intimam innumerorum illustrium amiciti- " am." Sammarth. Elog. p.83 and 4.—N.B. Though the Doctor rejected the *propositum sacerdotium* for himself, yet his Brother my Lord of Bangor was *made into a Bishop* by *fraternal* skill in the reign of Lord North.—Since this note was *first* printed, the public have lamented the lofs of this acute and very learned physician. *Dum loquimur* &c. &c. (July 1797.)

(*bb*) This allusion was evidently made since the 26th of Feb. 1797, soon after which the Bank issued the *One pound* notes, to the great disquiet of *the faculty.*

(*d*) "Siccat *inæquales* calices *Conviva Sacerdos.*" It is well known *by the Clergy* of a powerful diocese, that on public days when the *Claret or Burgundy* arrives at *a certain distance* from the top of the table, where *my Lord* is seated, the attracting power suddenly draws the bottles *across* the table. When avarice, pride, and meanness act upon the mind at once, I leave it to the metaphysicians to determine the curve in which it moves.—I say no more.

O'er *his* true church the crafty St. Pol (*e*) sleep, 195

Or bounds with Heretics John Milner (*f*) keep ;

Or

(*e*)_ The Bishop of St. Pol de Leon, to whom the chief care of
the public largess of this kingdom to the French Emigrants
sacred and profane is committed.   See the portrait of his Catholic Lordship in the public print shops of London.   It is impos-
sible to doubt the apparent propriety of the epithet I have given
him, if we only glance on the portrait.—I refer the reader to
all my notes on the Roman Catholic cause, in the Third Part of
the P. of L. It is indeed true that THE POPEDOM IS NOW FALLEN ;
but *the spirit of it*, I still maintain, is neither extinct nor asleep.
By way of *Contrast*, I cannot refrain from presenting to the reader the picture of Pope PAUL THE FOURTH, as drawn by the
master hand of Paolo Sarpi.   I will not injure the sublimity and
force of the language by a translation.   He well knew the court
and the policy of Papal Rome, and they knew him.   " E'ben
cosa certa, que PAOLO, come quello che era d'animo grande e
de' vasti pensieri, teneva per sicuro di poter remediare a tutti i
disordini *per la sola sua autorità pontificale*, ne riputava di *aver
bisogna* in ciò *di Principe alcuno* ; solito di non parlar mai con gli
Ambasciadori, *se non intonandogli nelle orecchie che* EGLI ERA SOPRA'
TUTTI GLI PRINCIPI ; che non voleva che alcuno d'essi domes-
ticasse seco, *che poteva mutar i regni*, che era SUCCESSOR *di* CHI
hà deposto Re et Imperadori." Ist. del Concil. Trident. Lib. 5.
This picture of a Pope, in the plenitude of pontific power, should
be presented to all Christian Countries " *in perpetuam rei memo-*
" *riam*," that they may contemplate what this spiritual tyranny
and usurpation once were, and what the principles of the Romish
Church sacred and political (which *never change* in essence, substance, or spirit under any calamity) will *at all times* naturally
introduce, whenever they obtain their full operation.   " *Ubi*
PAPA, *ibi Roma !*" in sæcula sæculorum! Let *England* look to
this.

Or Wilberforce range lawless through the town ;

I   Or

(*f*) To the revival of the Roman Catholic Cause in Great Britain, " *Pestis ero vivens.*" In our dread and natural horror of Atheism and of anarchy, why are *we* to revive superstition and tyranny ? I have nothing to do with the emancipation of the Catholics in Ireland, but to my apprehension it is a measure full of danger. It is at one stroke to alter the fundamental law and constitution of the country. I write in Great Britain, and direct my thoughts for this kingdom, wishing for *peace, tranquillity, and union* between the two Islands.—I have given more time and study to *this Roman Catholic subject* than any man perhaps, *at this time*, will think it deserves. I have perused many a dull and uninteresting tract, even of their own squabbles among one another, much to the loss of my own quiet. In general I pass them over and consign them to their own dulness. But there is one pamphlet, not for any even the least excellence of the composition but for the virulence of its spirit, which I call into public notice, if the public will or can feel upon the subject. It is entitled " A Reply to the Report published by the Cisalpine Club on the authenticity of the Protestation at the British Museum, &c. &c. by the Rev. John Milner," Printed for Coghlan, Duke Street, Grosvenor Square. 1795. It is written, as the title page informs me, by one JOHN MILNER, a Provincial Priest resident (*as I am told*) at Winchester, not an emigrant, nor in the King's House (while the Priests lived there *en masse*,) but the priest of a private chapel in that city. He seems by his writings, (I know no more of him) to be of the most intolerant principles *and deliberate* in the application of them. He exhibits at once the extremes of fierceness and of impotence. But he represents the opinions of *a very large* portion of their body by whom he is *accredited*. He is very cautious in this pamphlet, as he thinks, but his caution speaks plainer language than the frankness of the most open declaration. " It is apprehended (he says) that the publication of

PART IV.   " the

Or Mingay be the glory of his gown;

Or Erskine cease from impotent grimace,   199

And his appeals to (*g*) GOD, his prime disgrace;

Or

"the facts in question *might prove detrimental to the Catholic In-*
"*terest* (observe the words) *on any* FUTURE *application to the Le-*
"*gislature.*" p. 36. We see this *wary* prieſt has not thought
proper to conceal that *they have* FURTHER *intentions.* He tries
the ground before him, but his steps are uneasy. The indulgence,
it ſeems, is not to *reſt here.* The lenity of our government naturally leads to other *demands.* With this clue in my hand, I have
little difficulty to paſs through the intricacy of this Romiſh labyrinth. In another part of Mr. Milner's " REPLY," his indignation rises againſt ſome expressions in the declaration of the
Catholics. We see the embers under which the fire is not yet
extinguished. He is afraid *we Proteſtants* should think that the
ſpirit of *his* church has ſuffered an abatement. " Thus to MY
"*judgment* (he cries out) am I and the whole Catholic Body, *with-*
"*out conſenting to it,* pledged in the face of the Legislature to
"*condemn* the wars of Charlemagne, *and* THE CRUSADE *againſt*
" THE INFAMOUS ALBIGENSES." p. 28. I hope we are all
children of mercy, trained and educated in the benevolence and
charity which Chriſt has taught and enforced, and if we have
read the hiſtory of that infernal and murderous perſecution of the
devoted Albigenſes, (whoſe *chief* crime was their determined opposition and resistance to the Papal tyranny†) what opinion or
what comment ſhall we form on this merciless Prieſt, who *after
the lapſe of centuries,* feels *the ſame* paſſions and *the ſame* thirſt of
blood againſt these innocent victims of popiſh and arbitrary violence. *Crimine ab uno* DISCE OMNÈS !

† The Albigenſes were a ſect of the Waldenſes, who had their rise in the
twelfth century. I know what *the malice* of their enemies has ſuggeſted
againſt

Or one mean cause the virtuous (*h*) Scott maintain,

Turn law to trade, or deem religion vain;

Or (*ii*) Rose with coy submission, modest grace,

Rise to explain his sinecures and place;

Or smirking Abbot from old statutes rest,   205

And his self-consequence with law (*i*) *digest*;

Or the Bank bow to Pitt's imperial creed;

Or Dramatists to *public trust* succeed.

Nor think, a Poet's name I lightly prize,

Taught by the muse and by her wisdom wise;   210

I 2 But

(*g*) Nothing can be more offensive, more injudicious, and in some instances more profane, than when *a Barrister appeals to God* for the truth of every assertion made in a court of law, and in many cases when the facts have been doubtful, and sometimes have been afterwards proved to be false. I call this *a prime disgrace*; and I hope no Barrister of ability will follow this flippant rash habit of Mr. Erskine, in the Court of King's Bench, which *we* have all so repeatedly witnessed. Mr. Erskine's own better sense and serious thought will restrain him in future. But public men must be told of their faults publicly.

(*h*) Sir John Scott, Attorney General.

(*ii*) George Rose, Esq. Secretary to the Treasury, &c. &c. &c. &c. &c.

(*i*) Charles Abbot Esq. M.P. the new *Digester* of the laws and the proposer of some useful regulations. The Profession are afraid he will *cut too close* in his Reports to Parliament. The little shrewd Senator will smile and smirk, if he is told so. I would by no means discourage or depreciate the labours of a scholar and

a very

against them. This is not a place to *discuss* history, but I refer the statesman to Thuanus L. 1. S. 16. Vol. 1. p. 221. Ed. Buckley. N.B. For their confession of faith, which was presented to King Francis the First, by the wretched remnant of these Albigenses, I refer the theological and political reader to Sandius's Hist. Eccles. It is an honour to their religion. Sandius's words begin. " A. 1544. Merindoliani et Capraricnses &c. existentesque *Reliquiæ Albigensium* sequentem fidei suæ confessionem obtulerunt Francisco I. Regi Galliæ, quam a majoribus quasi per manus acceperant, abhinc anno post Christi Incarn: 1200," &c. Sand Hist. E. p. 425.

But in the wane of Empires (mark the hour)

Vice and the sword consolidate all 'pow'r;

Laws pass their (*k*) bounds; few statesmen stand

erect;

All in their country's name, themselves protect;

The Constitution sounds in every speech,   215

The words an insult, and each act a breach;

The public hopes with public credit sink—

At *such* an hour, when men to madness think,

What is a Poet, what is fiction's strain?   219

Junius (*l*) might probe a Nation's wounds in vain.

As

a very fenfible man; but I recommend to him the attentive perufal of " The Memoirs of P.P." Clerk of the Parifh (*of St. Ste-
phen's*) who " with the fweat of his hands *did make plain and
smooth the dogs ears* throughout the great Statute Book, &c.&c."

(*k*) The violence, sedition, and daring wickedness of *times
like these* produce the necessity of *extending* laws and regulations,
and acts which are declared *temporary*, and called for by that
necessity alone. When the danger is passed, the Constitution
is again left to protect itself by it's ancient laws, if that danger can *now* or ever pass from us. This is what Octavius
seems to mean, by " laws *passing* their bounds," &c. in this and
the *following* lines; and in this sense I hope he will be understood.

(*l*) O magnâ sacer et superbus umbrâ!

Stat. Sylv. L. 2. Carm. 7.

Junius told the nation, that " a time might arrive, at which
" *every inferior consideration must yield* TO THE SECURITY OF THE
" So-

As from a diamond globe, with rays condense,

'Tis SATIRE gives the strongest light to sense,

To thought compression, vigour to the soul,

To language bounds, to fancy due controul,

To truth the splendor of her awful face,   225

To learning dignity, to virtue grace,

To conscience stings beneath the cap or crown,

To vice that terror she will feel and own.

But if in love with fiction still, at court

Present in verse some new Finance Report,   230

How taxes, funds and debts shall disappear,

Or in the fiftieth or five-hundredth year.

Or tread the maze of *picturesque* delight,

From Holwood paint with Pitt the prospect bright;

Without one " line of boundary " to speech,   235

The summit of *conceit* with Gilpin (*m*) reach;

                                                   In

" SOVEREIGN, *and to* THE GENERAL SAFETY *of the* State." Introduct. to Lett. 35. This is not the doctrine of Horne Tooke and the desperate French factions and seditious societies now in England.—JUNIUS had not *so learned* the Constitution of England ; nor has the Author of the P. of L. so learned it.

In *Desolation's* dread *partitions* felt;

With *dip* and *bole, grand masses, burst* and *belt,*

With *shudders tremulous* explore your way,

Through *plashy inundations* (*mm*) led astray,   240

Till tir'd and jaded with the coxcomb strains,

Homeward you steal. " through Surrey's (*n*) quiet

    lanes,"   —   Renounce

(*m*) I am under the necessity of making a strong remonstrance
against *the language* of MR. GILPIN's writings on Landscape and
the Picturesque. It is such a *sartago* or jargon of speech as is
wholly unnecessary, though we are taught to believe them appropriate terms. They absolutely appear in troops. *Dips—Boles—
Grand Masses—Belts—Bursts—tremulous Shudders—plashy Inundations—partitions of desolation—continents of precipice—*and a hundred
more, till the English language sets all English meaning at defiance.
These terms are not the *parcæ devorta* of Horace, but mere jargon
and foolish affectation. Dilettanti and Connoisseurs almost
blush to use them. A term or word may not be quite obvious
or easy, yet it may not be affected. But the rage of *Concetto* ad-
mits no " line of boundary," as these gentlemen love to talk.
To use the words of Shakspeare in one of *his own* plays; as it now
seems, (for Dr. Farmer and George Steevens, Esq. take from him
and give to him *just as they please*) " They absolutely make a
battery through our defenceless parts." Pericles Prince of Tyre,
Act. 5. Sc. 1.—Simplicity in language is first to be sought.
Strength and dignity will follow. Government, the arts, morali-
ty, and religion, are all concerned in it's preservation. MR. GIL-
PIN's works on other subjects have and deserve high approbation.
In all but the picturesque he seems as ready as any man to say,
" *State super vias antiquas.*"

Renounce all Gilpin's jargon, said or sung, 241
And talk of Nature's works in Nature's tongue.
But still keep *Method*.

AUTHOR.

Method?

OCTAVIUS.

Yes: 'tis plain, 245
Connection, order, *method* you disdain:
You write when in the humour, scarce exact,
The thoughts disjointed, nor the sense compact;
'Tis Conversation, not by rule and book,
I wish you would attend to placid (o) Cook; 250
From

(*mm*) *Anglicè*, " Fens."

(*n*) " Stealing through the quiet lanes of Surry," is an easy and happy expression (*cur non omnia?*) of Mr. Gilpin's. Observat. in the Lakes of Westmoreland, &c. Vol. 2. p. 268.

From science A to science B proceed,
I hate your zig-zag verse and wanton heed.

AUTHOR.

Your counsel's good: I'll lock it in my breast,
Like Mansfield, I ne'er *enter* (*p*) my protest:

But

(*o*) See a late Poem called "CONVERSATION" by W. Cook
Efq.—I have read this poem a fecond time, and upon *re*-confide-
ration, it appears to me ufeful and written in a gentlemanly style,
didactic, temperate, and by no means inelegant in the verfe or the
compofition. An attention to the precepts, however felf-evident,
is too much neglected. We all are fond of the converfation of the
table, or as Lucian happily calls it the Φιλιας μεσιτις Τραπεζα,
the οφειλομενη απολαυσις.* The leaft honour I fhall do to Mr.
Cook, is to drink his health in my fober cups, and fuccefs to
his focial endeavours to promote regulated pleafantry and the
manners of a gentleman.

(*p*) The great Lord Mansfield Chief Juflice of the King's
Bench, and his nephew the late very learned (*ci-devant*) Lord
Stormont, made a rule never to enter a proteft on the Journals of
the Houfe of Lords.

* Lucian. Op Ερωτες. p. 571. Edit. Bourdelot.

But say, a simple story shall I tell?   .   255

A MAN OF METHOD is the theme.

OCTAVIUS.

'Tis well.

AUTHOR.

There liv'd a Scholar (*q*) late, of London fame,

A Doctor, (*r*) and Morosophos (*s*) his name:

K   From

(*q*) When I am very particular in the defcription of a character, I·abftain from giving the leaft hint of a real name. "Quis ra-
piet ad fe quod erit commune omnium ?"or in Le Sage's language,
" *qui fe fera connoitre mal à propos ?*"   I only give this as *A Character*, and fay no more.

(*r*) The word and title of " DOCTOR" is miferably abufed.
Erasmus long·ago in an Epiftle from Louvain in 1520 to the ce-
lebrated Cardinal Campeggio, obferved with fome indignation,
" *Unde* DOCTORIS titulo gloriantur, *nifi* UT DOCEANT? Erafmi
Epift. Ed. Lond. Fol. p. 652.   I wifh this were written in large
characters over the door of the theatre at Oxford and the Senate
Houfe at Cambridge.

PART IV.

From all the pains of study freed long since,

Far from a Newton, and not quite a (*t*) Vince ; 260

In metaphysics bold would spread his sails,

And with Monboddo still believ'd (*v*) in tails ;

At anatomic lore would sometimes peep,

And call Earle (*x*) useful, Abernethy (*y*) deep ;

                       With

(*s*) *Morosophos*. Stulté sapiens.—But more presently of Dr. MOROSOPHOS, *the Man of Method*.

(*t*) A learned and useful Professor of Natural Experimental Philosophy at Cambridge. See his works.

(*v*) All the learned world knows *how* Lord Monboddo believed and still believes, that men had once *tails* depending from the *gable-end*, of their bodies, supposing them to go *upon all fours*. N.B. Dr. Johnson defines the *gable end* to be " the *sloping roof* of a building," and he gives a pleasant instance from Mortimer's Husbandry. " Take care that all your brick work be covered &c. without *gable ends*, which are *very heavy*, &c."

(*x*) James Earle Esq. Senior Surgeon at St. Bartholomew's Hospital, and Editor of the celebrated PERCIVAL POTT's Works. I have been informed that the notes which Mr. Earle has added are valuable ; nor would I pass in silence the treatises he has given to the world in his own name, the result of extensive practice and accurate observation.

With Symonds and with Grafton's Duke (z) would

A Dilettante in Divinity ;   266   [vie,

K 2   A

(y) A young Surgeon of an accurate and philosophical spirit of inveſtigation, from whoſe genius and labours I am led to
think, the medical art and natural science will hereafter receive
great acceſſions.

(z) The Duke of Grafton, the Chancellor, and John Symonds, L.L.D. Profeſſor of Modern Hiſtory in the Univerſity
of Cambridge, have both attracted the public attention by their
various *Hints* and *Obſervations* on Subjects of Scripture.—I will
alſo offer a remark or two, which are *new* to me, on a paſſage in
St. Paul's Epiſtles, if another Layman may be heard with indulgence. There is no particular conjecture as to the peculiar
meaning or force of the following paſſage of St. Paul in the Second Epiſtle to Timothy. " *The Cloak* which I left at Troas
bring with thee, and the books, but eſpecially *the parchments.*"
Ep. 2. C. 4. v. 13. I would hint, that this Epiſtle was written
from Rome when Paul was brought before Nero the ſecond time.
Εγραφη απο Ρωμης, ότε εκ δευτερη παρεστη Παυλος τω Καισαρι
Νερωνι. In the 22d Chapter of the Acts, Paul was tenacious of
the privilege of Roman Citizenſhip, and it proved of much advantage to him before the Centurion. It may be, and it is, a
matter of mere *conjecture,* whether he might be *required* to prove
himſelf a Citizen of Rome, when he was to make his defence.
Theſe *parchments* (μεμϐραναι) might contain ſome documents, or be a deed or diploma of ſome conſequence to the matter in queſtion. But as to *the Cloak,* there is ſomething more
particular. The *Cloak* in the original, is Φελονης, or Φαιλονης,
which is undoubtedly a corruption for Φαινολης, and it is ſo read

in

A special clerk for *method* and for plan,
Through science by the alphabet he ran.

He

in the Codex M.S. Bibliothecæ Cæfareæ Viennenfis. Φαινολης was *grecised* from the Roman word *Pænula*. This is no more than was done frequently in other languages and in other countries. Particularly when the feat of Empire was transferred from Rome to Byzantium, the lawyers of the Imperial Courts were obliged to *grecise* many terms of law; as Φιδεϊκομμισσαριυς for *fidei commiffarios*, Ρεπυδιον for *repudium*, (as in this paffage, " Ευλογως ἡ γυνη το Ρεπυδιον στειλειε· κτλ." Juftinian. Novell. 22.) Κηνσευειν, for *Cenfere*, Εξπεδιτον, for *Expeditum* or *Expeditio*, κομπρομισσον for *compromiffum*, and other words, as may be feen in Du Frefne's and other Lexicons, but in particular in a most fingular and fcarce Glossary by Meurfius.* And in the Eaft, *before* the acceffion of the Houfe of Timour, the *Arabian* language was prevalent in *Hindoftan*, when the Hindoo Rajas had Communication with the Mahommedan princes ; and it is remarkable, that the *Arabian* language is ufed technically in the Code of Gentoo laws. Ch. 2. S. 3. " That is a woman's property, during the *Ayammi Shaddee*," which is the *Arabic* term for *the Days of marriage*. The trial of Mahorajah Nundocomar for forgery before the Supreme Court of Judi-

* " Joannis Meurfii Gloffarium Græco—Barbarum, in quo præter vocabula quinque millia quadringenta, Officia atque Dignitates Imperii Conftantinop. tam in Palatio, quam in Ecclefia aut Militia explicantur et illuftrantur." Lugd. Bat. 1614.

He took, not e'en in thought inclin'd to rove,

A wife for regularity, not love;   270.

A

Judicature in Bengal, will furnish many singular instances.—
But to return to the Φαινολης or *Pænula*. I would observe that
when the Roman state degenerated into a monarchy, many Citizens laid aside the *Toga* and wore the *Pænula*, or the *Lacerna* in
it's stead. Augustus highly disapproved of this change in their
dress. He was, as Suetonius informs us, *indignabundus*, and gave
orders to the Ædiles on the subject : " Negotium Ædilibus de-
dit, né quem posthac in foro paterentur, nisi positis *lacernis*, toga-
tum consistere." Octav. C. 40. But the *Pænula* was still worn.
As the *Pænula* was so *specifically* a Roman garment and worn
only by Romans, St. Paul might wish, as a slight confirmation
of his point, to shew what was his customary dress. It may be
remarked, that the *Pænula* was a vestment, which the Romans
generally wore *upon a journey*. Juvenal observes in Sat. 5. " Multo
stillaret *Pænula* nimbo," and St. Paul says, that " he *left it behind
him* at Troas."—This is only written as a mere literary remark to
hint, that in the minutest passages of the Scriptures there
may be some meaning ; and that nothing can be so contemptible as a foolish and a profane ridicule on any passage in
the sacred writings, *founded on ignorance*. The present remarks are intended as a matter of some little curiosity. But I
think there is no passage in the Hebrew or Greek Scriptures
which will not at last admit of such an illustration or explanation,
I mean *philologically* or *critically*, as may put to silence the ignorance
of foolish men. Much general information is to be obtained from
Harmer's valuable and satisfactory Observations on the Scriptures, collected from Voyages and Travels in the East ; (four
volumes 8vo.) and from " Letters from some Jews to Mr. Voltaire."

A little architect in all his schemes,

Some say he had *a method* in his dreams.

Fond of his ease, his Travels were at home,

And Lum'sden(*a*)taught him to converse of Rome:

On Sundays at Sir Joseph's (*b*) never fail'd,   275

So regular, you might have thought him bail'd;

With

taire." A man of real erudition, who merits the esteem of his fellow-creatures, constantly keeps his knowledge, his reason, and his *prudence* connected indissolubly, or as it is well expressed by a philosopher, Εν συναρμογα αδιαλυτω κατα λογον αριστον. Plat. Timæ. Locr. de anim. mundi. Plat. Op. Edit. Serrrani Tom. 3. pag. 95.

(*a*) That ingenious and learned gentleman, ANDREW LUMIS-DEN, Esq. F.A.S. Edinb. has since that time *taught us all* in the most agreeable scholar-like manner. See " His remarks on the Antiquities of ROME and it's Environs, being a classical and topographical Survey of the Ruins of that celebrated City."4to.1797. It is a pleasing and most judicious performance of a Gentleman who appears to have enjoyed the united advantages of foreign travel, studious leisure, and polite company.

(*b*) Sir Joseph Banks, Bart. Knight of the Bath, President of the Royal Society, Privy Counsellor, &c. &c. has instituted a meeting at his house in Soho Square, every Sunday evening,

at

With Jones a linguist, Sanscrit, Greek, or Manks,

And could with Watson play some chemic pranks;

Yet far too wise *to roast* a diamond *(bb) whole,*

And for a treasure find at last a coal.　　　280

Would sometimes treat, was liberal of cash,

(Not your damn'd *(c)* dollars, or Bank-paper trash)

Then

at which the Literati and men of rank and confequence, and men of no confequence at all, find equally a polite and pleafing reception from that diftinguifhed Gentleman. Sir Joseph Banks is fitted for his ftation in the learned world not more from his attainments and the liberality of his mind, than by his particular and unremitted attention to the intereft and advancement of natural knowledge, and his generous patronage of the Arts.

(bb) The ingenious Mr. Tenant has fhewn, in a paper read at the Royal Society, that he can reduce a *Diamond* by evaporation *to Charcoal.* I hear Mrs. Haftings and other great poffeffors of diamonds have a kind of *Tenanto-phobia,* and are fhy of this gentleman. *A poor Poet,* like myfelf, who has neither diamonds nor any thing precious belonging to him, can only remind Mr. Tenant and the Royal Society of the old proverb, " *Carbonem pro Thefauro.*"

(c) This verfe was evidently written after the 26th of Feb. 1797, after the order of Council was fent to the Bank of England,

Then talk'd, like Indian *(d)* Rennell, rather long,

And would at times regale you with a song,

But seldom that ; in music though a prig,   285

The little Doctor swell'd and look'd so big;

Nay to Greek *(e)* notes would trill a Grecian ode,

In diatonic kind and Lydian' mode,

                    And

---

gland, when the whole nation was made to pafs *through the pil-lars of Hercules.*

(*d*) Major James Rennell, the great Geographer of India, ὁ πανυ. A gentleman to whofe accuracy and extent of know-ledge this country is confiderably indebted. But this has no-thing to do *with his converfation.*

(*e*) Dr. Morofophos, the man of method, was rather trouble-fome to his friends on this fubject of Greek Mufic. He wifhed to pafs for another Meibomius. But there is ftill reafon to think that he never faw the three hymns to Calliope, Apollo, and Ne-mefis, printed with the Greek mufical notes to which they were fung, at the end of the Oxford edition of Aratus in 1672 by Dr. Fell, or the more accurate copy of thefe hymns in Mr. Burette's Memoire on this fubject. Memoires de'l'Academie des Infcrip-tions Tom. 5.—Dr. Morofophos knew but little of the fyftem of the Lydian Mode in the diatonic genus. There is alfo reafon to think that he knew as little, as Bifhop Horfley, of the Προσλαμϐανομενος, the Υπατη υπατων, or the Παρυπατη μεσων, &c.

And then with Burney, as his fit grew warmer,

Convers'd of Stentor the great (*f*) *throat-performer*.

Banks (*g*) gave him morning lessons how to dress,

And Morgan (*h*) whisper'd courage and finesse:

A Poet too he was, not very bright,

Something between a Jerningham and (*i*) Knight;

He dealt in tragic, epic, critic lore,   295

With half, whole plans, and episodes in store,

Method was all; yet would he seldom write,

He fear'd the ground-plot wrong, or—out of sight.

L   At

(*f*) " STENTOR is celebrated by Homer as the most illustrious *throat-performer* of antiquity." Burney's Hift. of Mufic 4to vol. 1. p. 340.

(*g*) Sir Jofeph Banks, Bart. &c. I fpeak only of " *Morning* habiliments."

(*h*) Maurice Morgan, Esq. an ingenious writer, author of the pleafant *Extravaganza* on the *Courage* of Sir John Falftaff. Mr. M. is known to his friends by the name of *Sir John*. In his politics, he is of the *Lansdown School*.

(*i*) R. P. Knight, Esq. author of " The Progress of Civil Society," which *he calls* " a Poem."
PART IV.

At last THE DOCTOR gave his friends a work! 299
(Not verse, like Cowper, or high prose, like Burke,)
CHAMBERS ABRIDG'D! in footh 'twas all he read,
From fruitful A to unproductive *Zed*.

OCTAVIUS.

What then? for ever fhall we wildly stray;
And pluck each hare-bell in the flow'ry way;
Or void of judgment, fire or critic force,   305
Stoop to each golden apple in the course?
I never can with argument dispense;
Pope gave the verse, but Warburton (*k*) the sense.

AUTHOR.

'Tis true; by plan and syllabus (*l*) confin'd,
Knight thus compofes first the reader's mind; 310

To

(*k*) Octavius is right in fome degree. The commentary of
Warburton on Pope's moral Poems is peculiarly valuable, and
explains many feeming inconfiftencies. Pope thought fo himfelf.

To rouse attention is the poet's art,

Knight calls to sleep, and acts a civil part,

Save to his view when foul Priapus (*m*) rose,

He wak'd to lust, in stimulating prose.

But though that *Garden-God* forsaken dies;   315

Another Cleland (*n*) see in LEWIS (*o*) rise.

L 2

Why

(*l*) Par *classes* et par *titres*,

Dogmatizer en vers et rimer par chapitres,

Boileau Sat. 8. 115.

(*m*) Concerning Mr. Knight's Treatise on the Worſhip of Priapus, in addition to what I before ſaid (P. of L. Part I. v. 134. Note (*g*) I ſhall offer the ſpirited words of Clemens Alexandrinus, from his Λογος Προτρεπτικος εις τ8ς Ελληνας or "*Admonitio ad Gentes:*" " Ταυτα ὑμων της ἡδυπαθειας τα αρχετυπα, ἀυται της ὑβρεως ἀι θεολογιαι, ἀυται των συμπορνευοντων ὑμιν Θεων ἀι διδασκαλιαι·—Πανισκοι,και γυμναι κοραι,καιΜΟΡΙΩΝ ΕΝΤΑΣΕΙΣ ταις γραφαις απογυμνυμεναι :—Ηταιρηκεν ὑμιν τα ωτα, πεπορνευκασιν ὁι οφθαλμοι, ἀι οψεις μεμοιχευκασι. Ω ∂ιασαμενοι τον ανθρωπον,και το ενθεουτ8 πλασματος ελεγκει απαρξαντες! κτλ.—"Clem. Alex. Edit. Commelin. 1616, p.30.&c.—I now diſmiſs this odious Treatiſe on Priapus *for ever.*—N.B. The learned reader will recollect that Clemens Alexandrinus lived in the third century under Alexander Severus and Caracalla, was a native of Athens, and that the famous Origen ſtudied in his ſchool.

Why sleep the ministers of truth and law? -

Has the ftate no controul, no decent awe,

While each with each in madd'ning orgies vie

Pandars to luft and licens'd blasphemy?   320

                                        Can

(n) John Cleland, author of "The Memoirs of a Woman of
Pleafure."

(o) M. Lewis, Efq. M.P. author of " The *Monk* a Romance."
in 3 Vol. (Vol. 2. Ch. 6 and 7.) See my Obfervations at length
in the preface to this Fourth Part of the P. of L. pag. ii. and iii.—The
publication of this novel *by a Member of Parliament* is in itfelf *fo
ferious an offence to the public*, that I know not how the author can
repair this breach of public decency, but by fuppreffing it himfelf.*   I will give Mr. Lewis an extract from the ninth Book
of the Hiftory of Procopius, called the *Hiftoria Arcana* of the
Emperor Juftinian and the infamous Theodòra. The words
are thefe.
" Αλλο τε μοι ενδειν ηθυς περιμνημονευσαι τηδε τυ Ανθρωπυ ουδ'
ὁτιουν οιμαι. ' Απαντα γαρ αυτυ τα της ψυχης παθη ὑτος αν
αξιοχρεως σημηναι διαρκως ειη.   Επει ὁστις αλογησας την ὑπερ
των πεπραγμενων την αισχυνην, ὑκ απαξιοῖ τοις εντυγχανυσι
ξδελυρος φαινεσθαι, τυτω δη ὑδεμια παρανομιας αταρπος αξατος.
Αλλα την αναιδειαν αει τυ μετωπυ προξεξλημενος, ρᾳστα τε και
ὑδενι πονω ες των πραξεων τας μιαρωτατας χωρει." Procop. Hif-
tor. Arcan. Lib. 9. p. 46. Ed. Fol. Lugdun. 1623.—I wifh Mr.
Lewis may read and profit from this paffage.

* Or Mr. Lewis might omit the indecent and blafphemous paffages in
another edition; there is neither genius nor wit in them, and the work as a
compofition would receive great advantage. I wifh he may at leaft take
this advice.

Can senates hear without a *kindred* rage ?

Oh may a poet's light'ning blast the page,

Nor with the bolt of Nemesis in vain

Supply the laws, that wake not to restrain !

Is ignorance the plea ? since Blackstone drew 325

The lucid chart, each labyrinth has a clue,

Each law an index : students aptly turn

To Williams, Hale, judicious (*h*) Cox, and Burn;

Obscenity has now her code and priest,

While anarchy prepares the dire Digest. 330

Methinks as in a theatre I stand,

Mark vice with folly saunt'ring hand with hand,

With

(*h*) Samuel Cox Efq. of the Court of Chancery, the Editor
(at his leifure hours) of the Reports of Peere Williams. I am
not very converfant with *profeffional* law books, but a learned
perfon fhewed me Mr. Cox's mode of illuftration, and defired
me to confider it. I really think, it feems as a model for all
future Editors of Reports of former years. This plan is evidently the mode of a moft judicious underftanding and of a well-
read Lawyer.—Tranfeat in exemplum !

With each ftrange form in motley masquerade,
Featur'd grimace and impudence pourtray'd,
While virtue, hov'ring o'er th'unhallow'd room, 335
Seems a dim speck through sin's surrounding gloom:
As through the smoak-soil'd glass (n) we spy from far
The circling radiance of the Sirian Star,
Faint wax the beams, if strong the fumy tint,
Till the star fades, a mathematic point.   340

Sure from the womb I was untimely torn,
Or in some rude inclement season born,
The State turns harsh on fortune's grating hinge,
And I untaught to beg, or crouch, or cringe;
For me the fates no golden texture weave,   345
Though happier far to give than to receive:
Yet with unvaulting sober wishes blest,
Ambition fled with envy from my breast;

For

(n) " If the eye glafs be tincted faintly with the fmoke of a
" lamp or torch to obfcure the light of the ftar, the fainter
" light in the circumference of the ftar ceafes to be vifible,
" and the ftar (if the glafs be fufficiently soiled with fmoke) ap-
" pears fomething more like a mathematic point."
                    Newton's Optics. Prop. 7. Theor. 6.

For friendship form'd, in yon starr'd fields above
My Saturn's temper'd by the beam of Jove.　　350
'I cannot, will not, stoop with boys to rise,
And seize on Pitt, like Canning, (*nn*) by surprise,
Be led through Treasury vaults in airy dance,
And flatter'd into insignificance. (*o*)
I cannot, will not, in a college gown,　　　　355
Vent my *first* nonsense on a patient town,
Quit the dull Cam, and ponder in the park
A *six-weeks Epic*, (*p*) or a Joan of Arc.

I leave

(*nn*) As pofterity may know little of this young Gentle-
man, I fhall add, that Mr. Canning was firft an Eton boy,
then wrote a little book of Eſſays, went to college, was then
made M.P. and after fome tuition and inftruction from the ac-
complifhed George Rofe, Efq. &c. &c. &c. *made* one of the
Under Secretaries of State. (1797.)

(*o*) " Peffimum genus inimicorum *Laudantes.*" Tacit. I know
no man more qualified to be a Commentator on Tacitus than
the Rt. Hon. William Pitt.

(*p*) Robert Southy, author of many ingenious pieces of poe-
try, of great promife, if the young gentleman would recollect
what old Chaucer fay's of poetry,

" 'Tis every dele
A rock of ice and not of fteel."

He gave to the public a long quarto volume of epic verſes, JOAN

OF

I leave these early transports, and the calm
Complacence, and the softly trickling balm   360
Self-consolation sheds! more sweet than all
Burke felt in senates, or Impeachment's Hall;
Borne to that course, where thund'ring from afar
The great Auruncian *(q)* drove his primal car.

E'en now, when all I view afflicts my sight, 365
All that Horne Tooke *(a)* can plot, or Godwin *(b)*
        write;

                                        Now

of Arc, written as he fays, in the preface, in *fix weeks.* Had
he meant to write well, he fhould have kept it at leaft fix years.
—I mention this, for I have been much pleafed with many of
the young gentleman's little copies of verfes. I wifh alfo that
he would review *fome of his principles.*

(*q*) Lucilius, the founder of Satire among the Romans, is
ftiled by Juvenal (Sat. 1.) the "Magnus Auruncæ alumnus."
He was a native of Aurunca a town of ancient Latium in Italy.

(*a*) Mr. Horne Tooke, in the conclufion of his "Diverfions
of Purley," makes an apology for applying himfelf to fubjects
so trivial as grammatical difcuffions, in the year 1786. He
ufes the words of an Italian poet, which are very remarkable,
though they never have been much noticed.

        "Perche altrove non have
        Dove voltare il vifo,
        Che gli è stato interciso
        Mostrar CON ALTRE IMPRESE *altra virtude.*"

                                        The

Now when Translation to a pest is grown,

And Holcroft to French treaſon adds his own,

When Gallic Diderot in vain we ſhun,

His blaſted pencil, Fatalist, (*aa*) and Nun ; · 370

M

·When

The hour was however approaching, when *his countenance* was to be *turned* to *other* thoughts, and he was to diſplay *other* talents which had almoſt ſlept ſince the time of Junius. At the blaſt of the French Revolution, he awoke from grammatical ſlumber, and found that *other* enterpriſes awaited him. We have traced his proceedings till his trial at the Old Bailey for high treaſon, Nov. 4, 1794. His *plans* were UNFOLDED, and though he was acquitted, and " Execution was not done on Cawdor," yet it is not impoſſible that hereafter, after his deceaſe, some honeſt chronicler may be found,

> " Who will report (in private)
> That very frankly he confeſs'd *his treaſons*,
> Implor'd *his country*'s pardon, and ſet forth
> A deep repentance.".   (*Macbeth.*)

Till that hour arrives, I ſhall wait for the continuation of his grammatical reſearches, which are promiſed to the world, with the celebrated wish of the Satiriſt,

> Ut vellem *his potius nugis tota illa* dediſſet
> TEMPORA SÆVITIÆ !

From the abilities and uncommon erudition of Mr. Horne Tooke I dread much, and from the calmness and mildness of his converſation I should apprehend perhaps more. But as I think THE WHOLE KINGDOM is fully, and deeply, and solemnly, and unalterably impreſſed with the nature, the malignity, the extent, the influence, and the terror of the grand Revolutionary Principle, and the desperate fury of Reforming societies, and embodied factions, I trust Great Britain and her Ministers will never ſuffer the arm of justice and vigilance to remit or to relax it's energies.

(*b*) See my account of this weak and contemptible writer, William Godwin, and his *Political Juſtice*, in Part III. of the P. of L.—See alſo a future note in this part of the Poem.

PART IV.

When St. Pol (c) sounds the sacring bell, that calls

His Priests *en masse* from Charles's ruin'd walls;

When Thelwall, (d) for the season, quits the Strand

To organize revolt by sea and land;

Now, when our public vessel, as it rolls,   375

Is left to Miles, John Gifford, or John Bowles; (e)

                                     When

(*aa*) The names of his posthumous novels, translated for *our* benefit.

(*c*) The Bishop of St. Pol. de Leon, to whom the care of the French Emigrant priests is committed *en masse*. The reader may recollect they *were* maintained in the old mansion built by Charles the Second at Winchester.—The reader may be surprised, but he will find by the papers laid on the table of the House of Commons, on the 21st of December, 1796, that *no less* a sum than 540,000l. was issued in one year for French priests and Emigrants, *sacred and profane.*—See the Preface to the P. of L. Part IV.—Hear again the *titular* Bishop of Waterford the R. R. Dr. Hussey in his Pastoral Letter to the Catholic Clergy in his diocese, (London 1797, reprinted by Coghlan No. 37, Duke Street, Grosvenor Square). Speaking of the *total* Repeal of the POPERY Laws in Ireland, he *warns* those who *oppose* it in these terms. " THE VAST ROCK *is already detached from the* " *mountain's brow,* and *whoever* OPPOSES it's descent and removal, " MUST BE CRUSHED *by his own rash endeavours!*" pag. 10. Is the common sense of England and of Ireland *drunk?* Or if it hath slept, will it not *now* awake ? Can any man say that *the political* spirit of *the Roman Catholic Religion* is extinct, that it is dead, that it is dying ? This titular Bishop warns us plainly enough. He has rocks and mountains at command in his cause, and all the powers of nature in their gigantic admeasurements appear at his great bidding.

Οσσαν επ᾽ Ουλυμπῳ μεμασαν θεμεν, αυταρ επ᾽ Οσση
Πηλιον εινοσιφυλλον, ιν᾽ ΟΥΡΑΝΟΣ αμβατος ειη·—
ΚΑΙ ΝΥ ΚΕΝ ΕΞΕΤΕΛΕΣΣΑΝ! (Hom. Od. L. xi.)

(*d*) This indefatigable incendiary and missionary of the French Propaganda, *John Thelwall,* has now his *Schools of Reason* in country towns, &c. &c. Περισσως εμμαινομενος.

When Barristers (*f*) turn authors; authors (*g*) prate;

CHARLES Fox allegiance dares to calculate,

And with his sulph'rous torch relumes the pile

With unaverted (*h*) face, and ghastly smile;   380

(*e*) Mr. W. Miles, Mr. John Gifford, and Mr. John Bowles. Writers of a very different character in private and public life. I believe I have been *misunderstood in this respect*. I never ranked them *in the same class*, though I have placed them in the same line. So did Pope; "Not with the Burnets, Oldmixons and Cooks." No man ever conceived that Bishop Burnet could be classed with Oldmixon. This was mere political prejudice in Pope.—*I have neither prejudice nor partiality.* Whatever I know of Mr. Miles, I dislike and often detest, but I do not always dislike his writing, and his information is not unfrequently accurate and important in the present state of public affairs. Mr. Gifford is sometimes *spirited* in his reply to Mr. Barrister Erskine, and just in his remarks; but as a writer I think him deficient; he seldom knows *when to have done*. But if he will attend, he may improve, even into excellence. I read his work and confess myself both obliged and grateful for it. The intentions of Mr. Bowles and his love of order and government have always had my commendation.— An anonymous writer indeed of political ability and of no common eloquence gave to the public, "Considerations on " the state of public affairs at the beginning of the year 1796." Owen Piccadilly. It is much to be regretted that this author never continued his labours. But *my proposition* is this. The Public have never seen a full, perfect, sufficient, and energetic vindication of the Great Cause in which Great Britain and her Allies have engaged, delivered to the country under the known auspices of the Minister by a man of talents, eloquence, and knowledge. Surely it was a dignus Vindice nodus. I am of opinion, it was Mr. Pitt's duty; I am sure it was his interest and the interest of us all. At present we appeal to facts intelligible enough, whose eloquence cannot mislead. We cannot all hear the Minister's speeches in the H. of C. It will, I fear, be said to Mr. Pitt rather *significantly* at some time hence, "Had you done so, *Tuque tuis armiis, nos te poteremur* ACHILLE." Ov. Metam. L. 13. v. 130.

(*f*) Mr. *Barrister* Erskine.—See more of him and his pamphlet on the French war in a future note.

(*g*) I refer to the House of Commons.

When Transatlantic Emigrants can roam

But to return, and praise *our (hh)* English home;

Now,

(h) In ancient times among the Romans, when *the public ministers* of funeral obsequies *set fire to the pile, they turned aside their faces.*

Triste ministerium, subjectam more parentum

Aversi tenuere facem. (Virg. Æn. 6.)

Not so the Right Honourable Charles James Fox!

As Mr. Fox *loves Greek,* I will give my opinion of Mr. Fox's *tongue* and eloquence in Greek. I shall then say of it—
Η Γλωσσα πυρ, η φλογιζυσα τον τροχον της γενεσεως, και φλογιζομενη υπο της Γεεννης, ακατασχετον, κακον, μεστη ιυ θανατηφορυ. If Mr. F. would attend to this *Greek Author,* he might learn the καλη αναστοφη, and the πρωτης σοφιας. Even Mr. Fox may possibly read *what I say.*— As Mr. Fox is *now* (June 1797) *studying* Mr. Gibbon's History, he will find many an instructive lesson for his public conduct. Mr. Fox, *I know* cannot always *construe* Mr. G's *English,* and is in the habit of consulting his friends on the *meaning* of many passages and sentences; but without much success. That pleasant companionable Gentleman Mr. Dudley North M. P. for Banbury will confirm what I say.† I always feel an interest in Mr. Fox's studies, whether he is reading Gibbon, or *culling simples* on St. Ann's Hill with Aspasia, or poring on the Odyssey, in lamentation over his *departed* friends in the H. of C. in the old Bard's language,

Αρνυμενος ην τε ψυχην και Νοστον Εταιρων,

Αλλ'υδ' ως Εταρυς ερρυσατο, ιεμενος περ. Od. I.i.

But his Εταιροι or Friends are said to have left him *only on one*

account;

† Perhaps Mr. Fox may understand and *construe* the following sentence from the *luminous* Historian. " An aspiring candidate may be tempted *to* " build his greatness on the *public confusion,* but it is the interest as well as *the* " duty of the Sovereign *to maintain the authority of the laws.*" Gibbon, Vol. 7. p. 90. Ed. 8vo.

Now, when the French _defend_ us (*i*) in disgrace,

French swords, French fraud, French priests, and

       French grimace;

When England changes arms—at such a view 385

Muſt I find _method_, verſe, and patience too?

My verse, the thunder of a Patriot's voice,

Cries loud to ALL who ENGLAND make their choice,

" Throw wide that portal; let no _Roman_ wait, 389

" But march with Priestley through the _dextral_ gate."(*k*)

                           OCTA-

account; his good humour and ability having never forſaken him. The account is this, deep, ſhort, and full:

  " Επει Τροιησιεροv πτολιεθροv επερσε."

                       Od. l. 1. v. 2.

(*hh*) See Mr. Cooper of Mancheſter's Account on his return from America, and the Letters of some wandering Journeyman Weaver or Carpenter, I forget which, &c. &c. " _Impudens liqui patrios Penates,_ &c."

(*i*) I allude to the French Emigrant Regiments, enrolled in the _Britiſh_ army. Surely this is a meaſure of government unwiſe, unaccountable on any found principle, a proje& of deſperation, as one would think. Is this a time for _Engliſhmen_ to ſay,

  Mutemus clypeos, _Danaûmque inſignia_ NOBIS

    Aptemus.   (Virg. Æn. 2.)

(*k*) " Through the _dextral_ gate !"—My alluſion is this: In ancient times, the moſt frequented roads _to the city of Rome_ had _double gates._ They who came into the city paſſed through the left-hand gate; and _they who went out of the city_ took _the right-hand_ gate. See Nardini Roma Antica, L. 10. c. 9. When Pliny, in his Natural Hiſtory, in the Chapter _de Roma_, Lib. 3. c. 5, is ſpeaking of the gates of the city, he ſays, that _twelve_ of

                               the

OCTAVIUS.

Talk thus, e'en Horsley shall applaud: proceed

AUTHOR.

. The tears that Britain sheds, her wounds that bleed,
Call for a fost'ring hand, the balm of PEACE,
Not styptics, which the sanguine tide increase,

Such

the *thirty seven* gates should only be *numbered once (semel nume-
rari)*; the expreffion is odd, but it alludes to fuch of thofe
gates as were *double* in this fenfe. This was not unknown in
other Italian cities. The *Porta de' Borfari* at Verona (in the
opinion of the Marquefe Scipio Maffei, Verona Illuftrata,
Part 3) was in reality a twin or double gate, though it has been
miftaken by fome antiquaries for an arch of triumph —N. B.
In times like the prefent, I would *never fhut* thofe *double* gates in *any*
city, when the turbulent, difcontented, and factious wifh to
retire into *foreign* parts. We all remember, that Sir Arthur
Hazelrig, John Hampden, and Oliver Cromwell, *being ready to
fail for America*, were STOPPED *by order of Council!* Hume's words
are very ftrong and remarkable in this *lecturing* age. " They
(i. e. Hampden, Hazelrig, and Cromwell) had *refolved* for ever
" *to abandon their native country*, and fly to the other extremity of
" the globe, *where they might enjoy lectures* and difcourfes *of any*
" *length or form* that pleafed them." Mr. Hume adds, very fig-
nificantly, " The King had afterwards full leifure to repent this
" exercife of his authority." Hume's Hift. Vol. 6. p. 311,
Ed. 8vo. 1773.

Such as State-quacks, or Barristers expose   395

For fame and sale, and sleeping might disclose:

In state affairs all Barristers are dull,

And ERSKINE nods, the opium *(l)* in his skill.

Saw'ft .

(l) Erfkine.—Mr. *Barrifter* Erfkine is *famous* for taking opium in great quantities, (I have often heard him fpeak in praife of it) and if he proceeds in this manner, it is apprehended that *his faculties will die* of too large a dofe, of which there are *many* fymptoms already. Mr. *Barrifter* Erfkine has informed the public, that HE *has not the talents of a ftatefman*, which, in common with the kingdom at large, I readily admit as part of my political creed; though it is fo very plain, as hardly to be an article of faith. In his late *flimfy and puerile* " View of the Caufes and Confequences of the prefent French War," he comes forth to the public μαλα σοφιστικως και σοβαρως, to ufe an expreffion from Themiftius, but I cannot ftile him in the words of that orator, before the Emperor Conftantius, as Ατυφs μοιρας φυσει μετεχον, Ζωον sρανιον, εκειθεν δοθεν τοις τηδε εις επιμελειαν. (Themift. Orat. p. 3. Ed. fol. Harduini, 1684.) I pofitively *will not translate* this Greek, either *for the Barrister himself*, or the country members, or the *worthy* electors of the town of Portfmouth; but I shall leave it to be *rendered faithfully* by the Reverend Dr. Parr, or Mr. *Barrister* Erskine's language mafter. Indeed in this age we require nothing but, what we call, eloquence; though the term is miserably abused. But *such as it is*, eloquence in the political world is like charity in the Christian character, without it a man is counted dead. However, in ancient times, in one particular there was a great and essential difference from the present. Perhaps it may not be without ufe to hint or remind *some folks*, that in Greece and

Athens,

Saw'st thou, (or did my troubled fancy dream?)
High o'er yon cliff, in majesty supreme,   400
                                          Vengeance

Athens, " apud Greciam, in the opinion and triumphant lan-
" guage of Cicero, De Orat. L. 1. quæ semper ELOQUENTIÆ
" PRINCEPS ESSE VOLUIT, atque illas omnium doctrinarum in-
" ventrices *Athenas*, in quibus SUMMA DICENDI VIS et inventa est
" et PERFECTA;" in Greece and Athens, I say, Orators and Barristers were never permitted to make any *epilogus* or *peroration*
whatsoever in the courts of the law, or in the senate. " Epi-
" logos ILLI mos civitatis abstulerat," says Quintilian; (L. 10.
c. 1.) and from WHOM? *From* DEMOSTHENES. On which
passage the learned Turnebus observes, " *Non licebat* ATHE-
" NIS *affectum movere ac ne Epilogo quidem uti;*" and yet DE-
MOSTHENES appeared *under this restriction.* What think you,
Mr. *Barrister* ERSKINE? Have you ever read *his* pleadings *for
the Crown*, or against Midias, or Περι Παραπρεσβειας? How say
you, Mr. *Barrister?*—MR. ERSKINE *is always below his natural
size*, when he speaks in the House of Commons. I have too
often disliked the manner and the matter. But as he confesses
himself *no Statesman*, he should have spoken with more modesty
and deference on political subjects to those who are confessedly
statesmen in the esteem of the country. I will leave in Mr.
Erskine's ear the words which Demosthenes thundered against
Androtion. It cannot however be supposed for a moment that
I can mean to compare a Gentleman of distinction like Mr.
Erskine, with such a being as Androtion. I only give *the
words*, and Dr. Parr may translate them if he pleases.

" Ει ανδραποδον η Πολις; αλλα μη των αρχειν ετερων αξιουντων,
ωμολογειτο ειναι, ηκ ιαη:αι; Ανδρες Αθηναιοι, τας :Υβρεις ηνεχεσθε
τας Τητη, ας κατα την αγοραν υβριζεν, -Ϭοαν εν ταις εκκλησιαις,
επι τη Ϭηματος, δηλης και εκ δηλων καλων εαυτη Ϭελτιης και εκ
Ϭελτιωων." (Demosth. Orat. Κατα Ανδροτιωνος. Gr. Edit.
Benen. 1570. pag. 398.)   In

Vengeance his attribute, (and, as he trod,.

The conscious waves roll'd back!) the passing GOD,

That shook old Ocean's empire? from beneath

Strange threat'ning notes in hollow murmurs breathe

Hoarse through the deafen'd shrouds! But hush'd

    the blast,   405

THE TRIDENT IS CONFIRM'D: the dream is past. *(m)*

Oh, strong against ourselves, and raſhly bold!

No voice, as in the Hebrew fane of old,

From Britain's center to her utmoſt bounds,

From parting *(n)* angels in sad accent sounds: .410

        N   Paine

In conclusion, I recommend *to all perſons* who have *an itch* for writing or ſpeaking, in public or in private, *from* Mr. Barriſter Erſkine *down to* Mr. Dent and his dogs, to ſtudy with care the following paſſage from Lord Shafteſbury, in his " Advice to an Author." The words are theſe : " Where the harm would be of ſpending ſome diſcourſe, " and beſtowing *a little breath and clear voice* purely upon ourſelves, " I cannot ſee. We might peradventure be *leſs needy and more* " *profitable in company,* if at convenient times we diſcharged " ſome of our *articulate* ſound, and *ſpoke to ourſelves* viva voce, " *when alone.*" Advice to an Author, Sect. I. This anticipating remedy of *Soliloquy* the noble author preſcribes againſt the diſeaſe called " THE LEPROSY OF ELOQUENCE," which is now a Britiſh Epidemic. Mr. Barriſter Erſkine, as I have been informed, has been under a regimen for a long time to no effect, and a Committee of Phyſicians and Surgeons (appointed by the Houſe) who have examined Mr. Erſkine's caſe, and the ſtate of his blood, have *reported* it as their opinion, that this " Leproſy of Eloquence," with which he is infected, is like the Leproſy of Naaman, the Syrian, that it will *cleave to him for ever,* except he rigidly adheres to Lord Shaftſbury's anticipating remedy of Soliloquy, and abſtains from ſpeaking in *all* places but in the Court of King's Bench.—*Illa ſe jactet in aula* ÆOLUS!

PART IV.

Paine may blaspheme, and Tooke and Thelwall
    mourn,

Our Ark's as yet by hallow'd hands upborne!

I too

(*m*) Thefe lines were written and inferted here at the latter end of the month of May, 1797.
    Proh dolor! Imperium Pelagi sævique *Tridentis*
    Cui nunc forte datum!
A patriotic poet may be, I hope, in this instance prophetical:
" The Dream is paft."

(*n*) I truft that Great Britain is *yet* firm, and that the guardians of her laws and conftitution will ftand bold, undaunted, and with deliberate valour. My allufion in the verfe is this. After the profanation of THE TEMPLE at Jerufalem, under the Roman Emperor Titus, we read (it is recorded by their own Hiftorian) that the voices of guardian angels were heard at the dead of night, crying out through it's inmoft recefles, Μεταβαινωμεν Εντευθεν, " Let us depart hence!" See the Seventh Book of the Jewifh War, by Josephus, pag. 1282. Edit. Hudfoni Oxon. I recommend the perufal of the whole of that wonderful fection (Cap. 5. L. 7.) The Hiftorian, in fome parts of it, is fcarcely inferior in fpirit, language, and fublimity, to Æfchylus himfelf. Surely at this moft awful hour when, I am alm, tempted to fay, the moral and the natural world feem to be breaking up together, when the moft powerful European ftates and populo cities have been convulfed or overthrown, can we hear, without et emotion and without a kindred horror, what the Hiftorian calls the " Ρωμαϊκων ταγματων αλαλαγμος συμφερομενων, the των Στασιαςων πυρι και σιδηρω κεκυκλωμενων κραυγη? Can we red unmoved, Ουτε ηλικιας την ελεος, ετ' εντροπη σεμνοτητος! Λιμω μαρανομενοι και μεμυκοτες εις οδυρμε; και κραυγην ευτονησαν. Συνηχει ητε Πειραια και τα περιξ ορη, βαρυτεραν ποιεντα την ὁρμην. Σω θορυβε τα Παθη φοβερωτερα! κτλ."—I will make *no* apology for prefenting the learned reader with this paffage, as Longinus

would

I too will call, loud through the gathering storm,

Godwin (o) and Volney, (p) ruin and reform;

The

would say, "Ουτω μεγαλοι οι λογοι, και εμβριθεις αι εννοιαι. όλον σωματιον δραματιχον και εναγωνιον." (Sect. 9. de Sublim.) I expect his thanks and not his cenfure, if he is worthy to read it.

(o) GODWIN.—" Ecce iterum Crifpinus!" and I wifh I need not proceed with the line, " Et eft mihi sæpe vocandus " in partes, Monftrum nulla virtute redemptum."—In my note (p) of Part III. of the P. of L. v. 177, I thought I had taken leave of WILLIAM GODWIN; but he has again obtruded himfelf upon the public, and I, as one of the public, fhall give a few remarks on his late book, called " The Enquirer; or Re- flections on Education, Manners, and Literature, in a series of *Effays*." Of his Enquiry concerning *Political Juftice*, the au- thor differs in opinion from me. He declares, in his Preface to his *Enquirer*, that " An Enquiry *thus* purfued on Political Juf- tice, (i. e. as he, William Godwin, has purfued it), *is undoubtedly* " IN THE HIGHEST STYLE OF MAN !!!" But as I have given my opinion, I fhall fay nothing here.—I fhall take *but a few chapters* of his new book, for really I fhould fatigue myfelf and my reader paft all fufferance, if I were to go through with it. The fpirit and the manner is the fame in *all* thefe Effays. " The prefent volume," (i. e. the Enquirer) he informs us, (Preface, p. 8) " is prefented to the *contemplative* reader, not as " *dicta*, but as the materials of thinking, and that they are com- " mitted to his mercy." He adds, " that with as ardent a paf- " fion for *innovation* as ever, he, (i. e. William Godwin) feels " himfelf more *patient and tranquil*." This is pleasant to him- self

The Sophists unabash'd yet rear their head,　　415
Their colours gaudy, though but idly *(q)* spread.

　　　　　　　　　　　　　　Better

felf certainly, but whether his opinions and their confequences will promote *patience* and tranquillity in *other* men, is all that we are concerned to know and to expofe. He profeffes to write a moral work. It is mifcellaneous and unconnected, whatever he may think. I would premife there is a difference in con-fidering a moral and a mere metaphyfical Enquiry. In the latter it is juft and neceffary to take in all the parts of a fyftem to know it's efficacy and apparent truth; but in a *moral* work there is not the fame neceffity, and for this plain reafon. Mankind are *guided in their actions*, not by fyftem, but by fingle impulfes; by detached maxims, by aphorifms, by fentences, which have frequently the force of whole volumes. Whatever impels to action *fingly and by itself*, may be confidered alfo *apart*, and held forth either to approbation or to cenfure. For this im-portant reafon I fhall offer fome paffages from " The Enquirer, by William Godwin." The book perhaps has been read very little ; but it is publifhed and it may be read, and I am fure it ought to be criticized, not from it's excellence or the ability of the writer, but from the fubject matter. His firft Chapter or Effay is, " *Of awakening the mind.*" He begins with *so very wise* a fentence, that we are naturally prepared for *much instruction.* I have indeed been told, that Mr. Godwin's mother, like little Isaac's in Sheridan's Duenna, ufed to call him " *Little Solomon.*" What is this fentence? verbatim as follows : " *If* individuals " were *univerfally* happy, the fpecies *would be* happy !" Again : " When a child is born, one of the earlieft purpofes of his in-" ftitutor ought to be, to *awaken his mind*, to breathe *a soul into the,*

　　　　　　　　　　　　　　　　　　　　　" as

Better be dull than wickèd ; from the heart
The life-springs issue, and their force impart ;

Better

" as yet unformed, *mass* !" Whether the *mass* is the *mind*, or
the *mind* the *mass*, and at what time *the soul* is to be
breathed into the mind, is not quite clear ; but it is *very instructive*.
Mr. Godwin also thinks, that " it is *not* the absurdest of para-
" doxes to affirm, that *the true* object of juvenile education is *to*
" *teach no-one thing in particular*, but (the reader will be rather
surprised) to *provide*, against the age of *five-and twenty*, a mind
" *well regulated, active, and prepared to learn*." It is to be remembered, that the *general* education of mankind is confidered. If the reader's mind is not *awakened* by such an ala-
rum of nonsense, I think he muft be deeply intranced, as faft
as a modern watchman or Mr. Godwin himself, when he wrote
the chapter. Next comes Essay 2. " On the utility of talents."
From this we learn, in Mr. Godwin's *own* words, that " The
" only complete protection against the appellation of *fool*, is to
" be the possessor of *uncommon* capacity ;" and that " a *self-sa-*
" *tisfied, half-witted fellow* is the *most ridiculous* of all things."
This is also *very instructive*, and lets us into the secret of Mr.
Godwin's wits and his self-satisfaction. But I cannot think Mr.
G's instructions will " produce in his pupil or child (if he has
either) " *one of the long-looked-for saviours of the human race*." It
might perhaps produce another Anacharfis Cloots, the *Orator
of the human race*. Then come " The Sources of Genius"
in Effay 3. The sentiments are either so trite, or so absurd, or
so wicked, that it is difficult to choose. One of them I must
select.—Of the children of *peasants*, Mr. G. observes, " That
" at the age of fourteen the very traces of understanding are
" obliterated. They are enlisted at the *crimping house of oppres-*
" *sion*.

Better to write like Coulthurst; *(qq)* better preach
With Hodson's *(r)* voice, and sacred flow'rs of speech,

                                    , In

" *sion.* They are *brutified* by immoderate and unremitting la-
" bour. Their hearts are *hardened,* and their spirits *broken* by
" *all* that they *see,* all that they *feel,* and all that they *look forward*
" *to.* THIS IS ONE OF THE MOST INTERESTING POINTS OF
" VIEW in which we confider *the present order of Society* !!! It
" is the great *slaughter house* of genius, and of mind. It is *the*
" *unrelenting murderer* of hope and gaiety, of the love of reflec-
" tion, and *of the love of life."* (p. 16.) This it is, I suppose,
as this atrocious but foolish writer would call it, *to promote patience and tranquillity* among mankind ! Mr. G. has not yet done.
Essay the 4th is on the fame Sources. Here he proves too
much for himself. He says, " There is an insanity among
" Philosophers, that has brought Philosophy itfelf into discre-
" dit." (p. 19.) At the close of the eighteenth century, Mr. G.
speaking of the succession of events, and the manner in which
we acquire ideas, delivers this sentence seriously and philosophi-
cally, with a view to be *instructive,* as I suppose. " *If* any man
" was to tell me that *if I pull the trigger* of my gun, a *swift and*
" *beautiful horse* will immediately appear *starting* from the mouth
" of the tube; I can ONLY answer, *that I do not expect it,* and
" that it is contrary to the tenor of my former experience.
" But *I can assign* NO *reason* (!!!) why this is an event *intrinsi-*
" *cally* more absurd, *or less likely to happen than the event* I have
" been accustomed to witness. It may be *familiarly illustrated*
" to the *unlearned* reader, by remarking, that *the process of gene-*
" *ration,* in consequence of which men and horses are born,
" has *obviously no more perceivable correspondence* with that event,
                                    " *than*

In soft *probation* for a Foundling's gown,   421
To please some guardian Midas of the town,

Who

" *than it would have* for me to *pull the trigger* of a gun !!!" I pass
by the indecency of the illustration, that I may just hint,
what it is to be a philofopher, and *instruct the unlearned* in the
new way.   I am ashamed to analyse any other opinions in this
Essay ; but as Mr. G. is supposed by some to be " A man of
talents," I suppose also that Mr. G. has the properties of " A
man of talents," as he *himself* has declared them to be ; and
that " HE (himself) can *recollect up to what period* he was *jejune,*
" *and up to what* period he was *dull*.   He can call to mind the
" *innumerable* errors of speculation he has committed, *that*
" *would almost disgrace an ideot*." (p. 28.)   For my own part,
in the present instance, I have nothing to do with *recollection*.
Mr. Godwin and his book are *before me*.   So much for " *A man*
" *of talents*."   I cannot oppress the reader with all his desolating, unfounded, and silly opinions on all trades, professions,
and occupations, wholly subversive of the order of society, and,
as I believe, of any supposeable order of any regulated human
society. But if the reader wishes to be amused with the acmé or
height of absurdity and wildness, I earnestly recommend to him
to read Mr. G.'s account of " The Walk of a man of talents,
" (Mr. Godwin himself, for instance) and of a man without
" talents, (such as myself) from Temple Bar to Hyde-Park
" Corner." (p. 31 and 32.) It is really *refreshing* in the extreme.
Nothing can be superior to it, but his " Gun of generation"
just described, and his " self-tilling plough, without the in-
tervention of man," in his other book on Political Justice,
Vol. 2. p. 494. Ed. 8vo.—I will give Mr. Godwin's *own* ac-

count

Who gives his vote from *judgment* and from *taste*;
Better with Warner move with *measur'd* haste

To

count of this *famous* Walk, especially as the public are in the habit of observing all kinds of men and women too *between Temple Bar and Hyde Park Corner.* " The *chief* point of difference
" (says Mr. G.) between *the man of talents and the man without*, con-
" sists in *the different ways* in which their minds are employed
" during *the same* interval!!!" (This is the propofition, ludicrous.
and absurd enough of itself, but now let us hear *the proof* or illustration.) " They, (i. e. *the man of talents and the man without*) are
" *obliged*, let us suppose, to walk from Temple Bar to Hyde
" Park Corner. The dull man goes *strait forward*: he has
" so many furlongs to *traverse*.. He *observes* if he meets *any of*
" *his acquaintance*; he *enquires* respecting their health and
" their family. He *glances* perhaps at the shops as he passes;
" he *admires* the fashion of a buckle, and the metal of a tea
" urn. *If* he *experience* any *flights of fancy* (i. e. between Tem-
" ple Bar and Hyde Park Corner) they are of a *short* extent; of
" the same nature *as the flights of a forest bird* clipped of his
" wings, and *condemned* to pass the rest of his life in a *farm-yard.*
" On the other hand, the man of talents gives *full scope* to
" his imagination. He *laughs and cries.* Unindebted to *the*
" *suggestions* of the surrounding objects *his whole soul* is em-
" ployed!" (We are now to prepare *for the employment* of
the whole soul of a man of talents from Temple Bar to Hyde Park
Corner, and the reader will *observe* that he has enough to do.
La voici.) " He, (the man of talent) *enters* into *nice* calcula-
tions; he *digests sagacious reasonings.*" (All this is done between
Temple Bar and Hyde Park Corner.) " In imagination he

" *declares*

To lend *new pleasure (s)* to a pedant's ear,

O   Appeal

" *declaims or describes*, impressed with the *deepest* sympathy, or
" elevated to the *loftiest* rapture. He passes through *a thousand*
" imaginary scenes, *tries his courage, tasks his ingenuity*, and thus
" becomes *gradually prepared* to meet *almost any* of the *many-co-*
" *loured* events of human life. He consults *by the aid of memory*
" the books he has read, (N.B. a man of talents never reads in
" the streets), and he *projects* others for the *future instruction* and
" *delight* of mankind." (I always said Mr. G. himself *projected*
his book on Justice and this on Education *in the streets*; " Sic
tu *triviis, indocte* solebas.") *If* he *observe* the passengers, (the
" dull man only observes his *acquaintance*) he reads their
" countenances, conjectures *their past* history, and forms *a su-*
" *perficial* notion of their *wisdom and folly*, their virtue or vice,
" satisfaction or misery. *If* he observe the scenes that occur,
" it is with the eye of a connoisseur or an artist." (The *dull*
man above minds only *buckles and tea urns*.) " Every object is
" *capable* of suggesting to him *a Volume of Reflections*." Mr.
G. must mean *his own volume* now before me, called *Reflections*
on manners, education and literature.) " The time of *these*
" *two persons* in *one* respect resembles; it has *brought them both to*
" *Hyde Park Corner*. In almost every other respect it is dissi-
" *milar*." Here is the denouement or the Ευρηκα of *Philosopher*
GODWIN, and I have no doubt he thinks it *a discovery* in *Terra*
jam cognita, as he will allow the ground to be between Temple
Bar and Hyde Park Corner. I cannot say *the Parallel* is quite
in the manner of Plutarch, but it is *very instructive*. No man
can ever be again *at a loss* to know a man of talents from a man
without, *in the streets*. I had often been puzzled, till I met this
instructive volume of *Reflections.*—When the reader has considered this, and all the other parts I have produced, and thousands
I have omitted, he will remember that MR. GODWIN has *set himself*

PART IV.

Appeal to Bryant, nor his judgment fear ;

Better

up for a Legislator, a Reformer, a Philosopher, a destroyer of ancient prejudices, and a builder of new systems, a guide through the darkness of this world by the new light, and he expects the obeisance of mankind. I am sure, I cannot even conceive that any man or woman will worship BEFORE SUCH AN IMAGE of Democracy and Tyranny, whoever may sound *the cornet, sackbut or dulcimer* at the dedication. It is not an Image of gold: it is an image of *iron mixed with miry clay*. For my own part I will not move from my place at the *sackbut* of Godwin, or the united band of musicians of a French Nebuchadnezzar. This it is to instruct the world, to reform it, to make it happy. Mr. G. comes in such a questionable shape, that I know not when to finish my questions. I might go on chapter by chapter in this manner. Let any man look at his opinions, and the nature of his knowledge and his pretensions. I must copy two thirds (at the least) if I wished to express and to expose all that is reprehensible in this volume, or wicked, or ridiculous, or trite beyond belief. I would hold up Mr. G.'s own propositions, in his own words, to all persons who have understanding, and let them judge. Let them fairly decide whether his impiety be not *even less* than his folly, and the weakness of his understanding more visible than the plunging violence of his exertions. " *Dat operam ut* cum ratione *insaniat.*" Mr. Godwin is at best but a mongrel and an exotic: He is grafted upon the stock of Condorcet and the French rabble ; but he has not even the *raciness* of that teeming soil. English minds will not long bear the grossness of such an imposition. We are better and earlier taught than he wishes we should be. . Reason indeed disclaims Mr. Godwin; in eloquence, and good writing, (in spite of all his dogmatism) he knows nothing; and of the Belles Lettres nearly as much as can be attained, or rather *picked up*; in a

modern

Better to state-arithmetic be bred,   420

Tell Jacobins and Tories by the (*t*) head ;

Prove.

modern academy in some London Square, or at Islington. But
for Mr. Godwin we are to lay down Plato and Xenophon; for
him we are to relinquish Aristotle and Tully ; to him Locke
is to give way, and the simplicity and tempered humour of Mr.
Addison is to be lost in Mr. Godwin's *effusions*.—I really am fatigued with this man.   Nothing but the importance of the consequences and effects of his wild, weak, wicked and absurd
notions (I cannot dignify them with the name of *principles* or
αξιωματα) could have prevailed upon me to have wasted irre-
trievably so much of my time upon them.   From the period
when *Philosopher* HUME first garbled his neglected " Treatise on
Human-Nature," and published it in the form of Essays, and
set up, as it were, a kind of *slop shop* of morality in the suburbs
of Atheism, we have had nothing but Essays upon Essays,
till—we all know the consequence.   And last of all comes *Philosopher* GODWIN, and sets up *his trumpery shop* too in the same
quarter ; though he is willing to wait upon ladies and gentlemen at their own houses, with his " Gros paquet de toile *verte*†
" *& rouge*," upon the principles and practice of the celebrated
Fripier in Gil Blas, and pretty much with the same kind of justice.   He presents you with his second-hand suits, with his
" *habits de drap tout uni*," and his " *habits de velours un peu passés*,"
demands his *soixante ducats*, and then addresses you with the
same cool effrontery ; " *Vous êtes bien heureux qu'on se soit addressé*
" *à* MOI *plutôt qu'à un autre. Graces au ciel, j'exerce* rondement *ma*
" *profession* : JE SUIS LE SEUL FRIPIER *qui ait* DE LA MORALE.‡"
So much for *Philosopher* GODWIN, or LE PHILOSOPHE FRIPIER,
malgré sa morale!—To the learned world in particular (if they
have ever *drudged* through the works of Mr. Godwin as I have
done) I will address a few words from the second book of the
Pyrr-

† *Green* is the symbol of the *Irish*, and *Red* of French democratic factions.
‡ Gil Blas, Liv. 1. ch. 15.

Prove that no dogs, as through the streets they range,

Give

Pyrrhonic Institutions of Sextus Empiricus, as applicable to *William Godwin*, after all the observations I have made on his writings. " Εξομεν δι' ὁ ΤΟΝ ΑΝΘΡΩΠΟΝ ΤΟΥΤΟΝδιαχρίναι τέ απο των αλλων Ζωων, χαιΕΙΛΙΚΡΙΝΩΣ ΝΟΗΣΑΙδυνησομεθα." Sext. Empyric. Instit. Pyrrhon. L 2. C. 5.

(p) Volney.—See Part I. (v. 120, note *e*) of the P. of L. for an account of Mr. Volney's book, entitled, " Ruins, or a Meditation of the Revolution of Empires."

(q) " Mocking the air with colours idly spread."
Shakspeare's King John.

(qq) Coulthurst.—The learned and Rev. Dr. Coulthurst lately published a Sermon, Oct. 25, 1796, written with the best and most serious intention, but in a style and manner so very unadvised, as to furnish matter of ridicule to some minute wits, who actually *put it* into doggrel verse. All Doctors (and Bishops too) should remember it is one thing to preach and another to print and publish their sermons. It is also high time for BISHOP HORSLEY (qui au travers de toute sa pieté *n'est pas Auteur impunément*, et qui a la satisfaction d'arracher *les Voluptueuses aux plaisirs* ‡, et *d'affermir dans leur devoir des Epouses ébranlées* par des amans seducteurs ; though I cannot say, " qu'on trouve *ses homélies* et ses ouvrages *egalement* forts et *delicats*) it is high time, I say, for my Lord Bishop Horsley to remember that it was said of the Archbishop of Grenada, " Voila *un Sermon* qui sent furieusement l'Apoplexie." (Gil Blas. Liv. 7. C. 4.) I do not think that the *Archevêque* de Grenade (I beg pardon) plain *Bishop* Horsley *(for he never will be an Archbishop)* will appoint *me* to be his Secretary, or in the inimitable words of Le Sage, G. B. l. 7. c. 2. be desirous " avoir près de lui un homme (com-
" me

‡ See his *Magdalen Homily*, and his speeches in the H. of L. in cases of Adultery.

Give bone for bone in regular (*u*) exchange ;

Or

" *me moi*) qui ait de la literature, et une *bonne* main *pour mettre
au net ses homélies.*"—I may add, that *if* I should take a walk
through his *literary* grounds, I fear I should be found *damage-
feasant*; and *if* I were to enter *the premises* at Rochester or
Westminster, and be prosecuted for it, I should certainly direct
my counsel to plead a special " *Nil habuit in tenementis.*" (See
Lord Raymond's Rep. 1550.) For though his Lordship, as
Plaintiff, is but an *Assignee*, he may take advantage of *the estop-
pel*, for *it runs with the land.* See Co. Litt. 152. and Salk. 276.

(*t*) Hodson.—Put synonimously for any *popular* preacher at
the Asylum or *elsewhere.* It is really humiliating and degrading to the Clergy to preach *probationary* sermons, on any vacancy
of a chaplainship at any of the charitable foundations, before
such a set of judges. One is for voice and action, another for
what he calls learning, others for the tender passions, some for
appeals to reason, and others again love *logic* and close argument.
No Divine can satisfy such judges, but such a Doctor as is described by John of Salisbury, " Doctor sanctissimus ille Gre-
" gorius, qui *melleo prædicationis imbre* totam *rigavit et inebriavit*
" Ecclesiam !"—It is high time to put these affairs on a more
respectable footing for the Clergy. I think indeed, that the business, elections, &c. belonging to all hospitals, and all charities,
should be transacted *by a Committee*, of the Subscribers, *elected
annually.* The propriety of such a measure being generally
adopted in London, and near the metropolis, is evident; and I
wish this hint might be attended to by men of sense.

(*s*) See a Treatise lately published, entitled " ΜΕΤΡΟΝ
ΑΡΙΣΤΟΝ, or a *New Pleasure*, recommended in a Dissertation on Greek and Latin Prosody. (1797.)" It is without any
permission, and I think with considerable effrontery, dedicated

to

Or frame, with Marsh, strange theorems to try

Some

to Mr. Bryant in a style perfectly new. If almost every page
of this treatise were not sillier, wilder, and more extravagant
than the preceding, I might be tempted to take some notice of
it's multifarious contents. For they are very numerous indeed;
from the laws passed in King Priam's reign (*I beg Mr. Bryant's
pardon*) under his marine Minister when Troy was attacked
and *invaded* by the Grecians, down to the present French war
and the incomprehensible Cavalry Act under George the Third
of Great Britain. As it does not appear to me *possible* for this
Author (I use *his own* words in *his own* treatife) to "*put off the
"monkey and bring out the man,*" I shall say nothing further of
this farrago of learned nonsense.

(*t*) Mr. Burke gave it as his opinion in his "Two Letters
on the Proposals for Peace," (1796) that there are "400,000 politi-
"cal citizens in Great Britain, of whom 80,000 are pure Jaco-
"bins, the other four-fifths perfectly sound," &c. In this particular instance I shall only say of this great and venerable man,
what one of Dante's Commentators says on a paffage in the
Purgatorio: "Per verità, è un gran capriccio; ma in ciò segne il
"suo stile." Dante, Shakspeare, Milton, and Burke, all abound
in similar capriccios; but I will add Dr. Johnson's admirable
words: "He that can put *them* in balance with their beauties
"muft be confidered not as nice but dull, as less to be censured
"for want of candour, than pitied for want of sensibility."
Life of Milton.

(*u*) Here is another little *capriccio* of a man of no common
sagacity, the late Adam Smith on Finances. He says *seriously*
by way of illustration; "No body *ever saw* a dog make *a fair
"and deliberate* exchange of *one bone* for another with another
"dog."

Some manuscript's divine identity ; *(ψ)*

Better.

" dog." Smith's Wealth of Nations, Vol. 1. p. 20. Ed. 8vo. My dear *Adam*, this philosophy of yours is nearly of the same date as your ancestor's* in Eden, and I can only say in reply, " Who " ever *expected* to see a dog do so?"—We have all heard and read of that snarling sect, the *Cynic* Philosophy, and if we could convert dogs into philosophers, or what is harder still, philosophical propositions *into meat and bones*, (which I fear is more than most *Scotch* Professors can do) I should apply metaphorically the following lines from a celebrated Poet, a great observer of *human* nature :

I" So when *two dogs* are fighting † in the streets,
    With *a third dog* one of *the two dogs* meets ;
    With angry tooth he bites him to the bone,
    And *this dog* smarts for what *that dog* has done."

(ψ) A learned and ingenious Critic, the Rev. Wm. Marsh, (Translator of Michaelis's Introduction to the New Testament, to which he has added many valuable notes and illustrations) published in the year 1795 " Letters to Archdeacon Travis, on the subject of a Greek Manuscript in the Public Library at Cambridge, printed at Leipzig, but sold in London by R. Marsh, Fleet-street." The following theorem is so new, and so unparallelled, that I cannot help preserving it in this poem as a
                                                                literary

* In the *most extensively learned* book I ever saw, (for the size of it) and the best arranged, I mean the " Philosophia Generalis, &c. per Theophilum Gale," there is *actually* a Chapter " *De Philosophia Adami*." L. 1. C. 1. f. 3.—" A *Capriccio*!"

† i. e. For *a bone*, or for any thing which is an object of *fair and deliberate* exchange.

Better be White, though dubious (x) of my fame,

Or

literary curiosity, and as most of my readers, I dare say, never saw, or even thought such a theorem possible. I shall laugh hereafter at any man who tells me, that the chances *for* or *against* any thing are 100,000 to 1.

"*General Theorem*, by which *the identity* of Manuscripts *is determined*, from a coincidence in their Readings." (Letters, p. 70.)

If after a collation of Greek MSS. to the amount of any number which I will call *p*, the reading, A, B, C, D, &c. to the amount of *m* have all been found in any of these MSS. which I will call X,* but not one of them in any other Manuscript: moreover if other readings A, B, Γ, Δ, &c. to the amount of *n* have likewise been all found in the MS. X, but each of them in only one other Manuscript; further if a third set of readings to the amount of *r* is contained in the MS. X, but each of them in only two other MSS.; a fourth set to the amount of *s*, each of which has been discovered in only three other Manuscripts, and *so on* : in that case, if all these readings should afterwards be found in any one Manuscript, *the probability* that the Manuscript, in which they are thus found, *is the very identical Manuscript* from which they had been taken, *is to the chances of its being a different MS.* as,

$$P^{m+n+r+s+ \&c.}$$

——————— — 1 to 1."

1^m. 2^n, 3^r, 4^s, &c. &c. &c. &c.
I shall say nothing, but leave the mathematical and divine calculating reader *con la bocca dolce*.

* In Mr. Marsh's problem, a Hebrew character (Aleph) is used, instead of the Greek X which I have used, as the printer had not the Hebrew characters at hand.

Or wisely sink my own in (*y*) Homer's name;

Better to disappoint the public hope,   428

Like *Warton* driveling (*yy*) on the page of POPE, (*yyy*)

P   While

(*x*) See the learned and very ingenious (but rather declama-
tory) Sermons by Profeffor White of Oxford at the Bampton
Lecture. But in this, as in many other cases, it seems, "Garth
"did not write *his own* Dispensary."—I always thought the
charge ridiculous; yet learned men would write *about it and
about it.* Any thing will serve for a controversy. Enquire of
Meffrs. Ireland, Malone, and Chalmers, at the *Shakspeare Manu-
factory* in Norfolk-street, in the Strand.

(*y*) The Rev. Dr. Parr will best explain this verse. See his
sublime Apostrophe, "*Spirit* of Henry *Homer* ! &c. &c. &c."
Letter to Dr. Coombe, by an Occasional Writer in the British
Critic.

(*yy*) The Bookfellers may say in Sir Philip Sidney's words:
"What fools were we, to mingle such *driveling* speeches among
' (WARBURTON's) noble thoughts! (Sir P. S's Arcadia.")
        Pan etiam *Arcadia* dicat se judice victum.

(*yyy*) See the new edition of Pope's Works by *the Reverend Dr.*
JOSEPH WARTON, late Head-mafter of Winchester School. The
mildest words I can use are, "Tantamne rem *tam negligenter?*"
I praised (and liberally enough as some people thought) Dr. Joseph Warton's Common Place Book on Pope, in the First Part
of the P. of L. and I still think it entertaining. But when a learned

PART IV.   man

While o'er the ground that WARBURTON once trod,

The Winton Pedant shakes his little rod,

Content *his own* stale scraps to steal or glean,

Hash'd up and season'd with an old man's spleen, 440

Nor e'en the Bard's deformity can 'scape,

" His pictur'd person and his *libell'd* (z) shape ;"

                          Ah,

man appears as the professed Editor of the most distinguished and the most interesting poet of the nation, and when the public have been taught to expect the work as of great promise, we require something more *than mere copying his own old common place remarks* from one book, *to put them* in form of notes at the bottom of the pages of another. It is mere book-making, beneath the character of such a gentleman as Doctor Warton. It is to steal *from one's own self.* But the town is patient : " Marcus dixit, ita est." *But I will not say so.* When the ILLUSTRIOUS friend of Pope, WILLIAM WARBURTON, (sublime in all his exorbitances, dignified in sagacity and erudition, and great even in his occasional rashness and idle wanderings) condescended to become an Editor, I should have preferred re-printing his edition as it stood. The ingenious Winchester School-master might with propriety enough have corrected the press and added some *little anecdotes* and excerpta from his classics. What was beneath Warburton might suit Dr. Joseph Warton. I am indeed ashamed of this edition upon the whole. But as there is no other new edition to be had of an elegant form, type and paper, (and this is *very pretty)* many persons will desire to have it, and I am sure I will not refuse it a place in my library. Perhaps, I have said more than is necessary; but there will be persons enough to praise the

                          Doctor's

I

Ah, better to unlearn'd oblivion hurl'd,

P 2   'Then

Doctor's gleanings *from himself*. But I shall say more, at the end of the next note.

(z) Poets are often prophets. POPE little thought that, fifty years after his death, an ingenious Schoolmaster and formerly a writer of little Odes to Fancy, evening owls upon a tree, apostrophes to the twilight and such nonsense, would actually revive some " *imputed trash*," (perhaps) *not his own*, and actually give to the malignant curiosity of some folks, " His libelled perfon and his pictured shape." (Prol. to Pope's Satires, v. 353.) It is strange that Mr. Gibbon and Mr. Pope should have the same fate. *The figure* of Mr. G. has been presented to the world and to posterity by *his friend* Lord Sheffield (See Mr. G.'s Posthumous Miscellanies, 4to Vol. 1.) and Mr. Pope's contemptible appearance by the *kindness* of his editor.—I have many and great objections to this edition; but I shall only state a few. An edition of Pope is a fair and a very proper subject of criticism. I think the title page contemptuous : " With notes and illustrations by J. WARTON, D.D. and *others*." To include WILLIAM WARBURTON under the title of *others*, required an assurance equal at least to the trifling *dilettante* spirit of such a commentator as Dr. Warton. In this instance, " *temulentus* videtur." I have no personal partiality for Warburton ; he was long before my time : nor have I the honour (such I should indeed esteem it) of an acquaintance with Bishop Hurd, his venerable friend and compeer. But I was born to admire erudition and genius, and to vindicate them when they are insulted. Dr W.'s life of Pope is not well written as to the matter or *the manner*. The style is defective and often vulgar. I shall instance a passage or two. The perpetual vulgarism of the term " *our* author."—" Dennis pursued *our* author in bitter invectives, against every work he *gradually* published." p. 18. " After arriving at eminence *by so many capital* compositions, *our* author," &c. &c.—p. 24. " Which,

as

Then give to Perry (zz) what I owe the world

And

as an uncommon curiosity, *one* would have been glad *to have beheld.*" p. 11. " Dr. Warburton's defence of the Essay on Man *ultimately got him a wife* and a bishopric." p. 45. " Into what a *mass* has he *raised* and *expanded* so slight a *hint!*" p. 21. Dr. W. is fond of " *delicious* lines, and *delicious* passages, &c. I cannot specify more of them in this note. He commends Voltaire too often and too much. He is also perpetually praising the German Professor Heyne, who has *insulted* our English universities and public schools in his writings. Yet *we* have republished *his* Virgil and all his ponderous dissertations. Professor Heyne was originally a mechanic : he was not born to taste, and he never acquired elegance. His learning is without discernment. More embodied dulness or a heavier mass of matter than *his* Virgil I never saw. The shrine of the Poet is indeed loaded with offerings, but it is illuminated with rays from *Gottengen.*—I must observe further. It was very bold and *very indecent* in the *Reverend* Dr. Warton, to publish Pope's Imitation of the Second Satire of the first Book of Horace. Pope never † printed it in his works himself; Dr. Warburton refused to admit it ; no common edition whatsoever of Pope has admitted it. It is printed only in a vulgar appendix in two volumes. I have indeed no doubt it is by Pope. As to mere wit and point in the imitation, it is perhaps the best. But what then ? Mr. Pope's works are distinguished at least for *correctness* in taste and *morals* ; and are intended

for

† Dr. W. says, vol. 1. Life p. 56. " Pope *suffered* his friend Dodsley to " print it as *his* writing in one edition 12mo." I never saw it, but can believe the Doctor. Pope was undoubtedly ashamed of it. But if Mr Pope had actually described every nymph in the scraglio of *the pious Needham,* must *the Reverend Dr. Warton* publish such a poem *merely because Mr. Pope had written it ?*— This sixth volume of Dr. Warton's Edition should be reprinted and this scandalous poem omitted. With the Commentators* on Shakspeare, Pope, &c. of modern days there is no such thing as an invocation to " *Intermissa* VENUS ; for the Goddess has actually deserted her beloved Cyprus, " *In hos* ΤΟΥΆ *ρης ʃʃ.* (See Horace for the rest.)

" Te, Venus Regina, *pio* vocantum
" Thure WARTONI ET STEPHANI decoras
Transfer in ædes."

* P. of L. Part I.

And idly busy, in my choice perplext,   445

Throw years of labour on a single text,

Alike

for the *most general and the most unqualified* perusal. Dr. W. might as well have printed Mr. E.'s *Geranium* in his comments. or any other light and vigorous sally of a *very* young man, forgiven as such and forgotten, as the following lines, if the reader will believe they are printed IN POPE'S WORKS;

    " Or when a tight neat girl will serve the turn,
    " In errant pride continue * * * ? †
    " I'm a plain man, whose maxim is profest,
    " The thing at hand is of all things the best."

               Vol. 6. p. 51.—see also p. 49. worse still.

If Mr. Pope had often written *thus,* his works must have been consigned to the library of a brothel. *This* edition of Pope's works will be sent into every part of the civilized world. This will be so; and can it be said, that I speak without reason? Surely I am not pleading for public decency in vain. The Doctor at least should have dedicated this sixth volume to the Ladies—*of the Commons.* To *what other ladies* could I present this volume? Yet so it is: " Doctors rush in, where laymen *fear* to tread." But because Pope called this " *sober advice* from Horace," the Doctor thought there could be no harm in it. Dr. W. observes, " that *the first step* in the *literary,* as " well as in the *political* world is of the *utmost consequence,* &c." Pope's Life, p. 14 I would remind the Doctor of *the last step* § in *both* these worlds, which he seems to have forgotten.

                                 I shall

---

† I, though an anonymous layman, refuse to print the passage *in full,* which *the Reverend* Doctor Warton has printed and sanctioned *with his name* as *Editor of Pope's works*
       Nobis *non licet* esse *tam diserti*
       Qui musas colimus severiores.

§ I was surprised to read these words in vol. 4. p. 333. on the compliment Virgil paid to Cato. " A much *honester* passage (says Dr. Warton) is that in " which Virgil had the courage to represent his hero assisting the Etruscans " in *punishing* their tyrannical king, in the 8th book of the Æneid v. 494."
       Ergo omnis *furiis* surrexit ETRURIA *justis,*
       REGEM AD SUPPLICIUM præfenti marte REPOSCUNT."
Dr. W. knows that Julius Cæsar was not Mezentius. I am sure the Doctor cannot approve and recommend a passage which has been in the mouth of every modern Regicide from the murder of Charles I. to the murder of Louis XVI. But why perpetually call out these passages to public notice, why dwell upon the " morgue et grandeur des *Souverains,*" " the authorised type of a *Lion,*" &c. &c. (v. 1. p. 33.) in times like these? We all love liberty as well as Dr. W. but a wife and good man discerns the signs of the times. These are the *under-murmurings* of a spurious, bastard, half-republicanism. I like them not.

(Alike to me, encas'd in Grecian bronze,

Koran or Vulgate, Veda, Priest, or Bonze)

And lend to truth itself unhallow'd aid,

In all the rashness of a fcholar's trade,　　　.　　450

And fall like (*a*) PORSON.

OCTA-

Ishall not make any remarks on Dr.W.'s criticisms on Pope at present, they are often pleasing and curious and gratifying, but chiefly
taken from his old Essay. I cannot now proceed. As Quintilian
says,† *Nos* genera degustamus, non bibliothecas discutimus." But
as to the conclusion of *one* of Dr. Warton's notes on the Prologue to
the Satires, I can well conceive it to be *his own* case, and I can believe it may be applied with feeling. Doctor Warton says, " *We*
" read (or *he* will read) with more satisfaction, the

Αψ' ὁ πᾶις προς κολπον εὔζωνοιο τιθηνης·

Εκλινθη ιαχων·

" than *we* do (or than the Doctor will hereafter do)
" Τρις μεν ορεξατ' ιων, ΤΟ ΔΕ ΤΕΤΡΑΤΟΝ ἱκετο τεκμωρ
" Αιγας. κτλ." Vol. 4. pag. 55." Which last is the motto to
this Fourth and last Part of the P. of L. I can indeed easily conceive, that after Doctor Joseph Warton has read *these remarks*, he
will *shrink back like the child* in Homer, *from the grey-goose plume
nodding*§ *on the head* of the writer of this note, and prefer luxury and
repose on the deep *bosoms* of his *well-zoned nurses*, the London
booksellers. To them and to their *consolations* ‖ I leave him. I
shall prefer the *solutis* Gratiæ zonis to all the booksellers in the
world.

(zz) *Perry*, put synonimously for the printer of any factious
newspaper.

† Quint. Lib 10. C. 1.
§ Δεινον απ' ακροτατης κορυθος νευοντα γενοας.
Il. 6. 470.
‖ *Ang'icè* £ 500.

OCTAVIUS.

You may spare your pains,
He gives no ear to any modern strains,
Save those, by Oberèa (*b*) fondly sung,
What time Opano (*c*) trembled on her tongue.

AUTHOR.

(*a*) See Mr. Professor Porson's Letters to Archdeacon Travis, of which the world has now heard *quite enough.* Mr. Professor Porson, *you may begin again,* but pray don't write in Mr. Perry's *little democratic closet* for the wits at the Morning Chronicle office. It is beneath you; I speak seriously. I know your abilities.—It may do well enough for Mr. *Professor*† Richardson, that fair *Fugitive* and Highland Bard, if a *certain political Dramatist's* compotations *will leave him any abilities at all,* which I begin to doubt. What is genius, without a *regulated* life!

(*b*) See " An Epistle from *Oberea,* Queen of Otaheite, to Joseph Banks, Esq," (now Sir Joseph Banks) Mr. Porson's favourite modern poem, which he can say or rather *sing* to his friends. It is very ingenious, but rather too free; the versification is exquisite. I believe it is the only piece of modern *English* verse Mr. P. will read.

(*c*) *Opano* or *Tabano* was the manner in which the name of Banks was pronounced at Otaheite. But *in this learned language,* as Mr. Zachary Fungus says to his brother Isaac in the Commissary, " Pshaw! you blockhead, I tell you THE NAME " *does not signify nothing.*"

† I allude to the Probationary Odes for the Laureatship. Mr. R. it seems, *was employed* by Mr. Dundas on that occasion. How could any man mistake an English Barrister for the Scotch Professor, who has written so very ingeniously on Shakspeare's characters.

AUTHOR.

Censure or praise let others seek or fear :   455

Look at *my* verse ; whose superscription's there ?

Whose cause do I defend ? 'tis your's, 'tis mine,

The statesman's, or the peasant's ; in my line,

All find in me a patron and a friend,

Unseen, unknown, unshaken to the end :   460

Yes, from the depths of Pindus shall my rhymes,

Through this mis-order'd world, these lawless times,

Be heard in Albion and her inmost state ;

All that the good revere and bad men hate,

In spirit and in substance, as of old,   465

The Muse in her *Asbestos* (*cc*) shall enfold.

                                  This

(*cc*) I know not whether I need mention it, but it was an ancient Roman custom to wrap dead bodies, before they were placed on the funeral pile, in a cloth made from a stone called *Amiantus*, or *Linum vivum*, by some called the *Asbestos*, on which fire had no power. (See D'Aubenton Tableau Méthodique des Mineraux.p. 10. Edit.Par.8vo.1784.) N.B. Mr.D'Aubenton, a gentleman of amiable character and of great accuracy of mind, is *now* (1797) resident in Paris, advanced in years, and by *quietly yielding to* every revolutionary *torrent* in the republic, has escaped the general exterminating massacre of the active Citizen Literati in the hall of *French Justice.* " *His armis illa quoque tutus in aulâ.*"

This is my *method*.—Though I sometimes stray
From Euclid's rigid rules to fancy's way,
Yet have I mus'd on Granta's willowy strand,
The sage of Alexandria (*d*) in my hand,   470
And mark'd his mystic symbols; the severe
And cogent truths dwell in my reason's ear.
The Stagirite too I sought, and could divide
(No Scotchman near, no Gillies by my side)
His sober sense from pride of intellect,   475
What Locke confirm'd, or warn'd me to reject.
Thence soaring on the balanc'd wings of thought,
(As Kepler hinted, but as Newton taught)
My mind in calm ascension to the height
Of the world's temple, through th' abyss of light,
Mid wand'ring fires and every starr'd abode,   481
Explor'd the works and wonders of the GOD,
Who fix'd the laws of order, time and place,
In his own great *sensorium*, (*e*) boundless space.

Q   The

(*d*) Euclid.

(*e*) " DEUS, *in spatio infinito,* tanquam *in sensorio suo,* res inti-
me cernit &c. &c." Newton Princip. Schol. General. Sub. 6n.
PART IV.

(84)

The Chemist's magic flame, the curious sport   485
Amber first gave, would oft my fancy court,
Led through creation's consecrated range,
Each flower, and plant, and stem, with every change,
Of vegetative life *in order* brought,
I magnified Linnæus (*ee*) as I thought ;   490
But spurn'd unfeeling science, cruel tales
Of virgin (*f*) rabbets, and of headless (*g*) snails,

And

(*ee*) But not in the spirit of that silly man, who inscribed these words under the print of Linnæus: " DEUS creavit, *Lin-* " *hæus* disposuit."—There is more folly in the inscription, than any intention of impiety ; it is the mere rage of antithesis without reflection. But in this botanising age, it should not pass without observation to *all* naturalists.

(*f*) *Virgin* Rabbets.—I allude in general to all needless, and cruel experiments upon animals. All that breathe, and feel and enjoy the gift of life from their Creator are entitled to protection from man, under those limits and degrees which an honest and upright mind knows without being told. But in this place I particularly allude to an anecdote *related to me by a friend*, of a Paper read at the Royal Society in the course of the last winter (1797.) on the subject of generation. The animal, chosen for these savage experiments by the merciless Doctor, was the Rabbet. Decency and humanity alike forbid the exposure of the process, and the mutilation of the parts of generation, before and after the animal was impregnated, and I think, in one or two of them, before the cöitus. Surely to sit calmly and to watch with an

impure,

And through the realms of Nature as I trod;

Bow'd at the throne, and faw (*gg*) the pow'r, of GOD.

Q 2   In

impure, and inhuman, and unhallowed curiosity the progress of
the desires, and the extinction of the natural passions in devoted
animals after such mutilations and experiments, is a practice
useless, wicked, foolish, degrading, and barbarous. There is
no justification to be offered. The mystery itself is not to be
disclosed to man. But we will know every thing; I wish, we
would recollect that we must account for our knowledge.
When an experiment, for any purpose useful to millions of our
fellow-creatures, has been once made upon an animal, it should
be *finally* recorded by men of science and veracity, as authentic
and satisfactory, not to be repeated. Sometimes, *as I was told*,
the idea of the cruelty exercised upon these animals was for a
moment lost in the ridiculous terms, which were perpetually
repeated in these papers, which occupied three or four sittings
of the R.S. *My friend told me*, that he actually thought that SIR
CHARLES BLAGDEN, KNIGHT AND SECRETARY to the R. S. had
been provided with specimens, and that he expected to see *Virgin*
Rabbets, *married* Rabbets, and *matron* Rabbets produced from
a basket on the table to lick, as in scorn and contempt, the very
mace of a Society who night after night could sit and hear
such a cruel farrago without indignation, but with half-smiles
and simpers at the *virginity* of these unprotected and devoted
miserable animals. When Papers are publicly offensive,
they should be publicly reprobated, and *not suffered to be produced* before the Royal Society upon a pretence of promoting
natural knowledge. WHY HAS THE SOCIETY A COUNCIL?
THE COUNCIL should be a literary and philosophical *Grand
Jury*. If it is not so, it is of no use whatsoever, but to gratify the
silly vanity of dilettanti noblemen and *busy* Baronets. I should
think Mr. PLANTA, the very learned, accurate, and well inform'd
Secr.

In morals, in religion, in the state,   495
In science, *without order*, ALL I hate.

OCTAVIUS.

I hear, not quite convinc'd : I honour still
Consistent excellence and measur'd skill ;
Not Extracts, (*h*) Beauties, pun, or anecdote,
Of social (*i*) Nicoll or young Cadell bought,   500

                               Such

Secretary to the R. S. would be of my opinion. To make such experiments as these, is to offer an insult to the *Sacrarium* of the Most High. For my own part, I would extend the famous speech of the Barons in the age of Henry the Third. I would thunder in the ears of the President and of the whole Royal Society, as a body, " *Nolumus Leges* NATURÆ *mutari !*"

(*g*) Here is another savage instance to no end or purpose whatsoever, but mere cruel sport of curiosity. The Abbé Spalanzani asserts that snails *re-produce their heads* after the amputation of the original capita. And he made experiments numerous beyond belief. But in the Academie des Sciences 1778, the reader will find Mr. Cotte differs from the humane Abbé, and says, " that *out of thousands of snails* who have *suffered* the operation, there have not been above *five or fix* of them, which have, as it is pretended, *reproduced their heads.*"

(*gg*) Νοημενα καθοραται·
                   St. Paul.

PART I.

Such pie-bald patchwork knowledge, as the bags

By Sappho wrought from scraps (*ii*) and colour'd rags.

    Yet speak, the hour demands : Is Learning fled ?

Spent all her vigour, all her spirit dead ?

Have Gallic arms and unrelenting war   505

Borne all her trophies from Britannia far ?

Shall nought but ghosts and trinkets be display'd,

Since Walpole *(iii)* ply'd the virtuoso's trade,

                              Bade

(h) Extracts, &c.—Constantine Porphyrogeneta, who was seated on the imperial throne of the Greeks in the 10th century, an age of much darkness, was the first person who employed the literati of his age in making *Extracts* from the works of the ancients. This employment has received it's consummation in *our* time, in all the Beauties, Anas, Elegant Extracts, Encyclopedias, Anecdotes, &c. &c. which have almost superseded the references to original writers, and created more half-scholars than the world ever saw before. It is however not without it's use, if judgment be exerted. It is rather singular that the very mode which was adopted for the revival of learning in the early ages, should be now followed with the opposite effect.—I am sorry that the Chief " *Public bag-man* " of the age, Mr. Seward, will not approve this note. I always approve his compilation in preference to all others.

  (i) Mr. George Nicoll, Bookseller to the King.

  (ii) A favourite amusement of the ladies at this time.

  (iii) The late ingenious Earl of Orford, Horace Walpole. The spirit of enquiry which he introduced was rather frivolous, though pleasing, and his Otranto Ghosts have propagated their species with unequalled fecundity. The spawn is in every novel shop.

Bade sober truth revers'd for fiction pass,   509

And mus'd o'er Gothic toys through Gothic glass ?

Since states, and words, and volumes, all are new,

Armies have *skeletons*, (*k*) and sermons (*l*) too ;

So teach our Doctors warlike or divine,

Simeon by Cani, or Wyndham on the Rhine.

Or has *Invention* slept ? the modern store   515

What Athens or Chaldæa knew before ?

All that the Gallic sage, with ill-starr'd wit,

Kens from his ancient (*m*) telescopic pit.

AUTHOR.

(*k*) The language of the House of Commons. It should have been in other terms. " Sunt lacrymæ rerum, et mentem mortalia tangunt." Sorrow is sacred, and should have the language of consolation even from the lips of a Statesman.

(*l*) See Claude's Essay on a Sermon with an Appendix, containing one hundred *Skeletons* of Sermons &c. By Charles Simeon, M. A. Fellow of King's College Cambridge. 1796.— This is as ludicrous and absurd in a Divine, as the term is offensive and unfeeling in Parliament during the miseries of war.

(*m*) See the " Origine des Decouvertes attribuées aux Modernes " 4to Par Monsieur DUTENS. 1797. The work is rather entertaining, but by no means encouraging, if *the Frenchman* did not generally substitute *conjecture* for *proof*. He observes page 130, in his tenth chapter, " that *the bottom of a pit*, from whence

PART I.   " we

AUTHOR.

All is not lost : (*n*) the spirit shall revive :   519
Lowth yet instructs, and Blayney's (*o*) labours live ;
With all who wander by the sacred fount,
(A chosen Band !) encircling Sion's mount,
Fast by the fanes and oracles of GOD,
And mark, with KING (*p*),where waves his awful rod.

                                    The

" we may see the stars at noon-day, may be imagined to be *the* " *primitive telescope.*" Mr. Dutens may sit in calm contemplation at *the bottom of his* ancient *pit*, and from that natural primitive telescope, see whatever best pleases his fancy ; for my own part I prefer the prospect from a cliff with the assistance of modern ingenuity, whether *invented* by Democritus or Dollond.

(*n*) I have in various parts spoken of those writers, who have done honour to Great Britain ; and it is not possible for me *to name all* those who, even now, form that constellation of ability and talents which has been or may yet be displayed, which Plutarch might call, in language somewhat lofty, (I think in his Treatise de placitis philosophorum) the Πολλων και συνεχως Αστερων συμφωτιζομενων αλληλοις ΣΥΝΑΥΓΑΣΜΟΝ.

(*o*) The deeply-learned Translator and Commentator on Jeremiah, &c. &c. B. Blayney, D. D. Regius Professor of Hebrew and Canon of Christ Church, Oxford.

The truth of evidence, the moral strain,   525

Nor

(*p*) As *The French Revolution and it's Consequences* must occupy and alarm the thoughts of every man who reflects, and stands in awe of the misery and desolation which have been brought upon the earth, and of the judgments which may be *yet* impending over Europe, I think I may be excused by many persons for the note which I am now writing. But first I recommend to all those who either ignorantly, or impiously, or presumptuously deny, reject, or vilify *the Scriptures*, to pass it over entirely. To them it will be foolishness. They have neither part nor lot in such a discussion. But under this restriction, and under this impression, I am inclined to extend the subject a little, and would call the public attention with much earnestness to some parts of a book printed in the beginning of the year 1788 in 4to, intitled " Morsels of Criticism, tending to illustrate some few passages in the holy scriptures upon philosophical principles and an enlarged view of things : by EDWARD KING, ESQ. 'F.R.A.S. printed for Robson and Robinson in 1788." The title of it is objectionable on every account, open to ignorant ridicule and unadvised ; but had a second edition of the work been called for, it might easily have been altered. The author of it appears to me, (I speak *from his book*) to be a gentleman of extensive erudition and ingenuity, and of accurate biblical knowledge, perhaps a little too fond of theory and some-times a little whimsical in his application of natural phi-losophy; but never without a serious intention and a pro-found piety. He never forgets *the nature* of the subjects he is treating. He seems to approach the sacred writings with that prostration of mind, that distrust of his own powers, and that self-abasement, which are *required* of those who desire to look into the hidden things of GOD. I speak of the spirit by

which

Nor HURD has preach'd, nor PALEY taught in vain;

R   Socinus

which he appears to me to be conducted, and (I repeat it) I
speak *from the work alone*. I shall contend for no interpretations
given by Mr. King or by any other man, but I may propose
them to public consideration. I never observed more caution and more wariness than in this writer. We know that it
is declared that " the book of prophecy is sealed *till the time of
completion;*" but the events of the world, of the Christian
world, are so awful and so alarming as to induce us to believe,
that they happen not without the immediate providence and
decree of the Supreme Being against the superstition and corruptions of man, and for the fulfilling of the preparation for
those times, when " the Kingdoms of this world must *(in
defiance of all human policy)* become the kingdoms of God and
of his Christ !" I will therefore offer to thinking persons some
passages from this work by Mr. King, *written several years before the present events* had taken place in Europe, or could be
conceived to be possible. I am as little disposed to superstition and enthusiasm as any man living; and I do not give
them as additions to the idle prophecies and random conjectures which have appeared in such numbers. I have too much
reverence for the reader and for myself on such a subject. But
the circumstance which peculiarly strikes me is this; that they
were written *without any specific reference* to any nation in Europe,
but simply and in general, that SUCH times and SUCH events
might be expected *in some part* of the Christian world. The first
passage I shall present, is a part of Mr. King's explanation of
the 24th Chapter of St. Matthew's gospel, principally of the
29th verse.† In regard to which he says, " We may remark,
" if the words are to be understood, as spoken merely emble-
" matically, then the images made use of are such as are well
" known

† Of course I refer the reader to th. book itself for the tenor of *the whole*
argument.

PART IV.

Socinus droops, and baffled Prieſtley flies,

And at the ſtrength of HORSLEY (q) ſhrinks and dies;

Nor

" known *to predict* (consistently with their constant use in many
" other parts of prophecy) *a great deſtruction and almoſt annihila-*
" *tion of many of those lawful powers which rule on earth,* however
" beneficial any of them may be to the earth ; *and* A DREADFUL
" LESSENING OF THE DIGNITY AND SPLENDOUR OF ALL
" GREATNESS, *and a subversion of all good. order and civil govern-*
" *ment.* Than which nothing can be expected more formidable.
" Dreadful indeed must be A TIME, *(if such an one is to come)*
" WHEN *men are let loose upon each other, possessed of all their present*
" *improvements and advantages, but unrestrained either by law and*
" *civil government, or by conscience and good principle ;* scorning the
" admonition and authority of those who ought to maintain juſ-
" tice, *and assisted by the more rude and barbarous parts of the world,*
" whom they shall find too ready to encrease THE UNIVERSAL
" UPROAR." Page 262—3.—At the conclusion of his Remarks
on the Revelations, Ch. 16. v. 13 and 14 he says : " *Here,* while
" we maintain *due reverential fear,* our interpretation must end.
" *Nothing but the events themselves when they come to pass,* can rightly
" explain the rest. And they will certainly *speak* LOUDLY
" ENOUGH *for themselves,* as those before have done —Only I
" must just remark, that *it seems,* as if *persecution* and the horrid
" influences of *superstition,* and of *ignorance* and of *barbarism* were
" allowed to produce their dire effects during *the firſt* part of the
" period of the time described *under the Vials ;* and as if, IRRE-
" LIGION, VANITY, AND A TOTAL WANT OF ALL SERIOUS
" PRINCIPLE, AND A MISAPPLICATION OF THE REFINEMENTS
" OF CIVILIZATION, *were to be* ALLOWED *to produce* THEIR MIS-
" CHIEF *also,* at the *latter* end of that period !" page 453. See
also, p. 456 and 57, which I could wish to copy, the words are

SO

Nor second stand in theologic fame

Sagacious HEY, (r) and RENNELL's (rr) learned
name,

R 2 And

so important, and the style so dignified. In the conclusion of
which Mr. King observes, *on the finishing of the mystery of God,*
" that as there should be false Christs and false prophets, so there
" should be also a dreadful subversion of all good government
" and order, and that. *men should be let loose upon each other, in*
" *defiance of all civil power and just rule,* and of legal restraint."
He subjoins some words too remarkable to be passed over. " *It*
" *will be happy for those who shall live some years hence,* if they can
" prove me guilty of a mistake in *this* point. I speak and write
" *with cautious reverence and fear;* acknowledging that I am
" liable to error, and *by no means pretending to prophecy:* but still
" apprehending myself bound not to conceal *the truth,* where
" any matter *appears to be revealed* in Holy Scripture; and es-
" pecially when the bringing *an impending d nunciation* to light,
" *(if it be a truth)* may be an awful *warning and caution* to
" many, AND PREVENT THEIR BECOMING ACCESSARY TO
" THE EVIL.*" Page 461. I must own, I am so struck with
these

---

* The following passage from the great Historian Josephus, on the inatten-
tion and ignorance of man in regard to the divine predictions, is remarkable.
The words are these :

Ταυτα μεν, ικανως εμφανιται δυναμενα την τ8 Θε8 φυσιν τοις
αγνοησιν, ειρηκαμεν, ὁτι ποικιλη τ'εστι και πολυτροπος, και
παντα καθ'ωραν απαντα τεταγμενως, ά τε δει γενεσθαι προλεγει·
την τε των ανθρωπων ΑΓΝΟΙΑΝ ΚΑΙ ΑΠΙΣΤΙΑΝ, ὑφ'
ἡς 8δεν προϊδειν εαθησαν των απ8βησομενων, ΑΦΥΛΑΚΤΟΙ
ΤΕ ΤΑΙΣ ΣΥΜΦΟΡΑΙΣ ΠΑΡΕΔΟΘΗΣΑΝ, ὡς αμη-
χανον αυτοις ειναι την εξ αυτων πειραν διαφυγειν !

Joseph. Antiq. Jud. Lib. 10. S. 3. p. 449. Ed. Hudson. Oxon.

And Douglas, (*rrr*) hail'd afar from earlieſt youth
Great victor in the well-fought field of truth.   530

HERSCHELL,

these passages, that *without any knowledge of* THIS ILLUS-
TRIOUS LAYMAN *but from his work*, I could *almoſt* address him
in the ſublime apostrophe of one of the moſt eloquent Fathers
of the ancient Church; " Ανθρωπε τε Θεε, πιστε θεραπον και
οικονομε των τε Θεε μυστηριων, Ανερ επιθυμιων των τε πνευματος, καλω Σε στυλον και εδραιωμα της Εκκλησιας, λογον ζωης
επεχοντα, και πιστεως ερεισμα, και πνευματος καταγωγιον." †
—Thus ‡ did this very learned and moſt pious man, in a strain
of serious, temperate, and impressive eloquence, deliver his
opinion and his interpretation. They will stand before us
and our posterity, as the memorial of that lonely wisdom,
that reverential application of the divine word, and of that
silent dignity, which can *alone* be attained by a retirement
(at intervals) from the world which God has made to HIM
alone, and by that worſhip in spirit and in truth, which when
joined to human erudition and to the sober cultivation of the
understanding, will produce FRUIT UNTO LIFE.—But I conclude; humbly acknowledging and deeply feeling myself wholly
unequal, and altogether unworthy, to speak of the awful sublimity of such subjects. My office can be but ministerial; it is
mine only to lead the aspirant *to the door* of the temple, and to
retire.

---

† Gregor. Naz. Orat. 19. (Op. Edit. Prunæi. p. 286. Paris 1609.) It was
pronounced before the great Basil, when seated upon the archiepiscopal throne
of Cæsarea. (A. D. circ. 374.)

‡ In the beginning of the year 1788, which were probably written many
years before they were offered to the public.

HERSCHELL, with ampler mind and magic glafs,
Mid worlds and worlds revolving as they pafs,
Pours the full cluster'd radiance from on high,
That fathomless abyss of Deity.

Who

(q) The Right Rev. Samuel Horsley, Bishop of Rochester. In my opinion the controversy so ably maintained by this Prelate, against the Herefiarch Priestley, is his peculiar praise. Bishop Horsley reminds me of the celebrated Divine, Charles Leslie. He has often the same strength, the same acuteness, and sometimes the same coarfenefs of manner. But the argument is cogent, the arms are irresistible. In theological controversy, Charles Leslie and Bishop Horsley always appear to me " *Æacidæ similes, Vulcaniaque arma capessunt*."

(r) The Rev. John Hey, D. D. late Norrisian Professor in the University of Cambridge. The arrangement, the learning, the accuracy and extent of his researches in theology, are conspicuous in his laborious and important work entitled " Lectures, &c." read as Profefsor.—N. B. The entire work is not yet published. (Oct. 1797.)

(rr) The Rev. Thomas Rennell, D. D. Author of a very able, learned, and eloquent *Apology for the Church of England*, preached in St. Paul's Cathedral, before the Sons of the Clergy, May 10, 1796.

(rrr) The Right Rev. John Douglas, D. D. Bishop of Salisbury, a Prelate whose erudition, penetrating sagacity, and well directed efforts have discovered and overthrown many strong

holds

Who in the depth abstruse of intellect   535
A greater now than WARING (*ss*) shall expect?
Lo, where Philofophy extends her fway,   —
Guides future Navies o'er the trackless way,
More voluble and firm ; so, strong in thought,
The royal Synod ATWOOD (*sss*) sate and taught. 540

                                        Who

holds of literary imposture. The names of Lauder and Bower are only remembered to their infamy.—The Bishop's Treatise on Miracles, called " The Criterion," should be reprinted. Why is it not again presented to the public? (Oct. 1797.)

(*s*) Dr. Herfchell's new doctrine concerning the *Materia Solaris*, has attracted much attention among the learned. I offer to their consideration a curious passage, which I met with when I was reading with a very different purpose. The *Platonic* PROCLUS, in the third book of his Commentaries on the Timæus of his great Master, mentions that Aristotle (whom, surely with justice, he calls ὁ θαυμαστος Αριστοτελης) hints, that neither the Sun, nor even the Stars, are *absolutely bodies of fire*. The words are these: " Τον των Αστρων χορον, και αυτον τον μεγαν Ηλιον, ΟΥΚ ΟΝΤΑ ΕΚ ΠΥΡΟΣ." *Procli Comment. in Timæum Platonis*, Edit. Basil. Gr. 1534. page 141. There is another fingular passage (not so explicit as this from Proclus) in the first book *de Cælo* of the Second Ennead of *Plotinus* the Platonicorum Coryphæus, as he has been called : he talks also rather quaintly from Aristotle of a " Πυρ τη των Αστρων προσφορον φυσει." Plotin: Ennead. 2 L. 1 page 99, &c. Edit. Basil. cum Comment. Ficini.—The reader is referred to Dr. Herfchell's most curious paper. " On the Nature and Construction of the Sun and Fixed Stars." Phil. Trans. Part I. 1795.

Who may forget thee,(*t*)BEATTIE? rustic(*v*)BURNS,.
And all his artless wood-notes Scotland mourns.
With England's Bard, with COWPER, who shall vie?
Original in strength and dignity,
With more than Painter's fancy blest, with lays
Holy, as saints to heav'n expiring raise. (*x*)   546

High

(*ss*) Edward Waring, M. D. Professor of the Mathematics in the University of Cambridge.

(*sss*) See a Paper in the Philos. Trans. 1796. Part I. entitled " The Construction and Analysis of geometrical propositions determining the positions assumed by homogeneal bodies which float freely and at rest, on a fluid's surface, also *determining the stability of ships* and other floating bodies, by GEORGE ATWOOD, Esq. F. R. S." The R. S. presented Mr. Atwood with their medal on this occasion.—The names of *Herschell, Maskelyne, Cavendish, Woollaston, Milner,* &c. dignify the Royal Society. We have yet some "Master Builders in the Sciences," as Mr. Locke once expressed himself.

(*t*) James Beattie, L. L. D. Author of " The Minstrel, 2 books." It is to be *for ever* regretted that this true Poet and most excellent man never finished his exquisite Poem. My mind dwells upon it, particularly on the First Part, even from my boyish days *at school.*

(*v*) Robert Burns. The Ayrshire Ploughman. An original Poet.

(*x*) William Cowper, Esq. Author of " The Task."—Τοω Μυσαων ιερη δοσις ! Such are the words of the divine Ascræan, in his *Theogonia.* Of *these* Muses seated on *our own* Parnassus, it may be said,

" *There*

·High from the climes of Latium's happier day

The Muse on ROSCOE (*xx*) darts her noontide ray,

And with each soft, each reconciling pow'r,

Sheds gleams of peace on MELMOTH's (*xxx*) closing

    ' hour ;   550

                             Bright⁻

     " *There* did they sit, and do their holy deed,
     That pleas'd both heav'n and earth !"

               Bishop Hall's Satires. B. 1. S. 2.

The conclusion of the Poet's work is so sacred, so dignified, so unequalled in simplicity and unaffected piety, that I hope none will read it without those sensations and without that improvement it seems designed to inspire.

     " But all in HIS hand whose praise I seek,
     In vain the Poet sings and the world hears,
     If HE *regard not*, though divine the theme.
     'Tis not in artful measures, in the chime
     And idle tinkling of a minstrel's lyre,
     To charm HIS ear, who looks upon the heart :
     Whose frown can disappoint the proudest strain,
     Whose approbation—prosper even mine."

                                 B. 6.

    (*xx*) William Roscoe, Esq. the historian of Lorenzo de Medici called the Magnificent. See the P. of L. Part III. at the conclusi n.

    (*xxx*) WILLIAM MELMOTH, Esq. a most elegant and distinguished writer, " near half an age with every good man's praise." His translation of Cicero and Pliny will speak for him, while

                                   Roman

Bright to the goal in their sublime career

BRYANT and BURKE (*v*) the torch triumphant bear;

S While

Roman and English eloquence can be united. Mr. Melmoth is a happy example of the mild influence of learning on a cultivated mind, I mean of that learning which is declared to be the aliment of youth, and the delight and consolation of declining years. Who would not envy this " FORTUNATE OLD MAN" his most finished translation and comment on Tully's *Cato?* or rather, who would not rejoice in the refined and mellowed pleasures of so accomplished a gentleman and so liberal a scholar.

(*v*) It is to be wished, that these TWO GREAT MEN may *now conclude* their political and literary labours. " *Finem dignum et optimo viro et opere sanctissimo faciant!* Quintil. Lib. 12. Cap. 11. —Since writing the above, when I heard of the death of that UNEQUALLED man, the Rt. Hon. EDMUND BURKE, ‡ I could only say to my friend,

Η μαλα λυγρης

Πευσεαι αγγελιης, ἡ ɥκ ωφελλε γενεσθαι,

Κειται ΠΗΛΕΙΔΗΣ!

Such was my veneration for this Great Man when living, such is the depth of my homage and the secret affliction of my spirit at his departure. It appears to me expedient and grateful, that we should all remember and revere THE MAN, to whose *primal* exertions (it cannot be repeated too frequently) we *originally* owe the publick sense of the moral, political, and religious danger of England from the grand *crushing* Cabal, grounded and rooted in France, and branching out and overshadowing all Europe.† I speak, as I think, in sincerity. Without much reflection we cannot understand the *full* nature and extent of the publick obligation to Mr. Burke. I would not vindicate any man from the cradle

to

‡ July 1797.—See Mr. Burke's character, in " *The Imperial Epistle from Kien Long, Emperor of China*, to George the Third of Great Britain," v. 117. page 10. Edit. 8vo. 1796.

† The *Abbé* BARRUEL has done a public service to Europe by his eloquent and perspicuous delineation of *the History of Jacobinism* in his work intitled " *Memoires pour servir à l'histoire du Jacobinisme.*" I by no means subscribe to *all the Abbé's* opinions and particular doctrines, or to his *whims* and fancies. But in the disposition of the whole work I perceive the hand of a master. He has discovered and traced from the very source the original Cabal, and its impious infamous leaders; and he has laid down their scheme, and disposed the proofs

PART IV. from

While Granta hails (what need the Sage to name?)

Her *lov'd* IAPIS on the banks of Cam. (*vv*)

But

to the grave ; much less a politician and a statesman. The very
region of Politics is baneful; it is too frequently " the soil the
Vices like." Every statesman, in or out of power, knows his own
meanness, the turbulence of his passions, the rattles of office,
the irritation of opponents, the jealousy of rank, and the impa-
tience of consorted power. All this is true. But still, when I
have revolved the various labours of EDMUND BURKE, and THE
CAUSE HE HAS MAINTAINED, (as it regards government, religion,
and society, not the details of the war and it's conduct) I say, with
this allowance for the feverous frailty of the passions, and the
taint of mortality in all our best actions, I would record in lasting
characters, and in our holiest and most honourable temple, the
departed Orator of England, the Statesman, and the Christian,
EDMUND BURKE !—" *Remuneratio ejus* CUM ALTISSIMO !"

(*vv*) I wish, (and every *Etonian* and every member of the
University of Cambridge *of good character* will join me heart and
hand) that this great, disinterested, virtuous and CONSUMMATE
Scholar and Physician, *now* by learning and religion conducted
with

from their own authentic writings and works, in a convincing, orderly, and
logical arrangement. It is worthy to be read by all who are interested in the
great cause of GOD and man, and I hope it will be read and studied. It is
the best historical and critical commentary extant (except the events themselves) on Mr. Burke's first work, called " Reflections on the Revolution in
France." 1790.—It is for such paramount reasons, that the Legislature and all
the Magistrates of Great Britain are loudly called upon *to controll* (while they
yet can controll with effect) *by the law and by the law alone*, such works as
those by Thomas Paine, and all the spawn of lewdness, infidelity and democracy in their vigour or in their dotage ; to repress *by law* such popular
works or novels as THE MONK, by M. Lewis, Esq. M.P. which I have stated †
amply, as indecent and blasphemous ; and to watch over the proceedings of
Dr. Geddes ‡, the new Translator of the Bible. The plain questions are these :
" ARE WE TO BE PRESERVED? and, " CAN WE BE PRESERVED?" The
French Revolution is *now* matter of history. I mean of History speaking in
every language of *every* nation of Europe. One establishment upholds another;
and the fall of any one draws after it *a long Ruin*. Read the Memoires of the
Abbé BARRUEL, and doubt, if you can, whether LITERATURE has power
to kill and to make alive. Atheist Statesmen always co-operate with Atheist
Philosophers, but are generally duped by them. " *Ils prennent leurs ordres sans
le savoir*," said D'Alembert, in the plenitude of his impudence. The grand
triple Conspiracy and *crushing* Cabal, under all its horrid formularies, against
religion, regal power, and social order under moral restraint, has shewn what
is the force and potency of LITERATURE stimulated and conducted by an exterminating philosophy. LET ENGLAND BEWARE AND LOOK TO HERSELF !

† Preface to Part IV, of the P. of L. p. 2, 3, 4, 5, & 6.   ‡ Ib. ib. Pref. to P. IV.
p. 19, &c.

But whence that groan? no more Britannia sleeps,
But o'er her lost Musæus (*xx*) bends and weeps. 556
Lo, every Grecian, every British Muse
Scatters the recent flow'rs and gracious dews
Where MASON lies; he sure their influence felt,
And in his breast each soft affection dwelt,   560
That love and friendship know; each sister art,
With all that Colours, and that Sounds impart,
All that the Sylvan theatre can grace,
All in the soul of MASON "FOUND THEIR PLACE!"

Low sinks the laurell'd head; in Mona's land   565
I see them pass, 'tis Mador's drooping band,
To harps of woe in holiest obsequies,
" *In yonder grave*, they chant, OUR DRUID *lies!*"

HE (*v*) too, whom Indus and the Ganges mourn,
The glory of their banks, from Isis torn,   570
In learning's strength is fled, in judgment's prime,
In science temp'rate, various, and sublime;

S 2   To

with dignity to the close of life, may be known by this affectionate verse *to all posterity*, "*The lov'd* IAPIS *on the banks of Cam.*"

    " DIIS DILECTE SENEX, te Jupiter æquus oportet
Nascentem, et miti lustrârit lumine Phœbus.
Atlantisque nepos; neque enim *nisi charus ab ortu*
Diis superis poterit magno favisse poetæ.
Ergo ego te Cliûs et magni nomine Phœbi
MANSE PATER, *jubeo* LONGUM *salvere* PER ÆVUM!
            MILTON AD MANSUM.

To Him familiar every legal doom,
The courts of Athens, or the halls of Rome,
Or Hindoo Vedas taught; for him the Muse 575
Distill'd from *every* flow'r Hyblæan dews ;
Firm, when exalted, in demeanour grave,
Mercy and truth were his, he lov'd to save,
His mind collected, 'gainst opinion's shock
JONES ftood unmov'd, and from the Christian rock,
Cœlestial brightness beaming on his breast, 581
He faw THE STAR, and worshipp'd in the Eaft.

Thou too, OCTAVIUS, that dread hour must feel,
Nor eloquence, nor wit, nor patriot zeal,
Nor piety sincere without the show, 585
Nor every grace Pierian pow'rs bestow
From pure Ilyssus and the Latian shore,
What Swift, or great Erasmus felt before,
May save thee !—yet, yet long, so friendship calls,
May guardian Angels hover round the walls, 590
Where love and virtue fix their blest abode,
Friend of thy country, servant of thy God ! (*yy*)

Octavius,

(*xx*) The Rev. William Mason, M. A. author of Elfrid'a, Caractacus, Musæus a Monody on Mr. Pope, The English Garden, &c. &c. &c. &c.
(*y*) SIR WILLIAM JONES. One of the Judges of the Supreme Court of Judicature in Bengal, &c. &c. &c. &c.

Octavius yes, it is, it shall be mine,

With praise appropriate still to grace my line :

To me all heedless of proud fashion's sneer,   595

MAURICE (z) is learn'd, and WILBERFORCE sincere,

(Though

(*yy*) In this *political* and *depressing* period, it is some comfort to divert the attention for a moment to such characters of literary and poetical excellence as The Rev. William Mason, and Sir William Jones—and to be able to add *my own* Octavius. OCTA-VIUS OPTIMUS, are the legitimate words of Horace. With an allowance for the partiality of friendship, (and who that ever felt such an affection will refuse to grant it) and with sorrow that *now* he must *neither be understood nor named*, I assert with truth, that OCTAVIUS is form'd to move among the highest and the foremost in the state, though contented and submitting to act in a station, certainly not without honour, yet inadequate to his faculties.—" *Exornet ætatis nostræ gloriam !*"

(z) *The Reverend* THOMAS MAURICE, Author of " Indian Antiquities, in 6 vol. 8vo." and of " the History of Hindostan, " it's Arts and it's Sciences, as connected with the History of " the other great Empires of Asia, during the most ancient " periods of the world." Vol. 1. 4to. is only yet published. The public is well acquainted with their merits. But it is with the most serious concern, that I read what Mr. Maurice has de-clared in his dedication, that " *This History* commenced under the " patronage of the Court of East India Directors, is dedicated to " them, *in humble hopes of their continued support of a work*, which " MUST SINK WITHOUT THAT † SUPPORT."—Learning has felt a degradation from these words. I believe that WILLIAM PITT, the *first* Earl of Chatham, would have wrested such a Scholar as

Mr.

† The E. I. Company subscribed for a certain number of Copies. This is not patronage.

(Though on his page (*a*) some pause in sacred doubt)
As Gisborne (*b*) serious, and as Pott (*c*) devout.

For

Mr. Maurice from the hands of the Merchants, and placed him under the direct patronage of the Crown. But the name of *William*,(though Erasmus in one of his Epistles§ once dwelt upon it with satisfaction,) is no more connected with literature. The present Minister, the Rt. Hon. William Pitt, (though he holds the second high office in a learned university) in this respect, can only be delivered down to posterity, " as a negative instruction to his successors for ever." But I neither call upon Nabobs, nor Directors, nor Ministers with the same earnestness, or with the same censure, as upon the Guardians and Bishops of the Church of England. It is to be remembered, that the whole tenor of Mr. Maurice's writings is to establish the truth of Christianity in general, as well as of some disputed doctrines, from the very sources whence some of it's adversaries have drawn arguments against it. The Archbishops of Canterbury and York, the Doctors Moore and Markham, the Bishops of London, and Durham, and Winchester, Porteous, Barrington, and North, are called upon to confer support and dignity on such a distinguished champion of the truth of the cause. If they neglect it, without an adequate reason, I affirm, they are guilty of a breach of duty to the kingdom, and to the establishment they are appointed to uphold. When I argue with Bishops on such a topic, I suppose they acknowledge the force of a *moral* obligation, and I cannot allow myself to think I suppose too much. " A dispensation is " committed unto them." Οικονομιαν πεπιστευνται. I speak with firmness, I am sure I mean to speak with respect. I am sorry, to say, they have not often such an opportunity. I speak not to *intrude* upon the Bishops, but to point out to them a gentleman whose promotion would be a matter of satisfaction to the learned.

I am

§ Epist. *Gulielmo* Budæo. Erasmi Opera Edit. opt. vol. 3. Part I p. 184.
Ep. 203.

For Athens CUMBERLAND (d) seems born alone ,

To

I am not to be told, that researches like those of Mr. Maurice are
liable to the caprice of erudition, and of uncertain application,
and that his style, matter, and manner are frequently too luxu-
riant and diffuse. The foundation of a temple may be strong,
though every ornament on the pillars may not be just.—I never
saw MR. MAURICE in my life; nor am I in the least acquainted
with him but by his writings and character. (June 1797.)

(a) See, "A Practical View of the prevailing religious system
of Professed Christians in the higher and middle classes in this
country, contrasted with real Christianity." By WILLIAM
WILBERFORCE, Esq. M. P. for the county of York.—Some very
serious persons have their doubts as to the theological principles
of this work in their *full* extent, and I fear it is sometimes *too
rigid and exclusive* in it's doctrines. There is also too much of
a *sectarian* language, which cannot be approved. But of the
intention, virtue, learning, and patriotism of the eloquent and
well-informed Senator, I have the most honourable and decided
opinion. His work is vehement, impassioned, urgent, fervid,
instant; though sometimes copious to prolixity, and in a few
parts even to tediousness. Perhaps it is the production of an
orator rather than of a writer. Throughout the whole, there
is a manly fortitude of thought firm and unshrinking. But
for my own part, for obvious reasons, I dislike the term,
"*Real* Christianity," as *exclusively* applied to any *set* of propositions drawn from the Gospel. If I regard *external* circumstances, I would not indeed take theology from Athanasius or
Bossuet, morality from Seneca, or politics from Lansdown or
Syéys. But I will own, that from a scrutiny into the publick
and private character of Mr. Wilberforce, I am inclined to
think that his enemies would be *forced* into an acknowledgment,
(as it is recorded in the words of a prophet), that "they can

find

To bid her comic Patriot be our own;

Nor

find no occasion against this man, except they find it against him concerning the law of his God." A reader of his work must be good or bad *in the extreme,* who may not receive some advantage from the awful composition. I am indeed unworthy to praise it, and I feel myself so. If I may descend from divinity to *mere* philosophy, I shall add, that if Mr. Wilberforce proceeds and acts upon the sublimity of such principles, we may apply to him the expressions drawn from the fountain of Plato by his most enthusiastic votary, Plotinus. " Αφ'
" ἑαυτȣ μεταϐαινει, ὡς εικων προς αρχετυπον, τελος εχων της
" πορειας!" He will best comprehend the high and holy sentence which declares what is the life of such men; " Ουτω θεων και ανθρωπων θειων και ευδαιμονων ϐιος, απαλλαγη των αλλων των τηδε, ϐιος ανηδονος των τηδε, ΦΥΓΗ ΜΟΝΟΥ ΠΡΟΣ ΜΟΝΟΝ!" Plotini Ennead: 6. L. 9. c. xi.

(*b*) The Reverend Thomas Gisborne, M. A. Author of an Enquiry into the Duties of Men, &c. and of the Female Sex, &c. &c. eminently entitled to the public esteem and gratitude.

(*c*) The Rev. J. H. Pott, M. A. the learned and excellent Arch-deacon of St. Alban's. In his writings instructive, laborious in his office, and exemplary in his profession.

(*d*) Richard Cumberland, Esq. an author of various talents, and of very considerable learning. It is scarcely necessary to enumerate his compositions, in particular his dramatic works, which have received the sanction of publick esteem. In my opinion he has done very great service to the cause of morality and of literature. He is author of a work called "The Observer," and from the translations in that work of the fragments of the Greek comic writers, I believe all learned readers will agree, that he is the only man in the kingdom (with whom we are *publickly* acquainted) equal

Nor yet ungrac'd may SULIVAN (b) remain,

Serene in fancy; nor in science vain,

Yet still, though oft his various works I scan,

I quit the volume, when I find the man.

Good books (b) are the mind's bread : (excuse the

phrase,   605

Gifford will bear the term, and Cowper praise)

T   They

equal to the translation of Aristophanes. I wish it were to be the amusement of his retired hours. I shall never think he has been "public too long;" but as he has quitted *the* stage, (as he affirms himself,) such a translation would be an easy, yet an adequate and honourable, employment for a man of unquestionable genius, versatility of talents, knowledge of the world, and a *consummate master* of the poetical language of our best ancient dramatic writers. Let us hope that Aristophanes may yet be our own.

(a) RICHARD JOSEPH SULIVAN, Esq. F.R.S. and F.A.S. author of " Philosophical Rhapsodies, &c. and of a work entitled " A View of Nature, in Letters to a Traveller among the Alps, with Reflections on Atheistical Philosophy now exemplified in France, in six vol. 8vo." Printed for T. Becket, Pall Mall. A work of labour and of general utility, digested from original writers with judgment and with an upright virtuous heart, in a pleasing and instructive manner. I dwell with affection on such a character as Mr. Sulivan; and, if this were the place and if India were the theme, I might make honourable mention of the works and excellence of his Brother, JOHN SULLIVAN, Esq.

(b) It is pleasing and satisfactory to think that *all* books which are absolutely *required* to strengthen, exalt, purify, and inform the understanding, and consequently to correct and en-

PART IV.   large

They give the life-blood, nutriment and health,

And laugh to scorn the insolence of wealth.

OCTA-

large the affections and the heart, are of easy access and of
easy price. With the luxury of learning and the modern elegance of types and paper, I have nothing to do, but *earnestly
to deprecate all needless extravagance and brilliant folly in new
publications,*‡ if they are defigned to be of service to the world,
and to be purchased. The august and sublime monuments of
religion and of genius may be adorned without blame, or rather
with great commendation. When the Bible, Shakspeare, and
Milton appear in all the splendour of typographic art and the
magnificence of decoration from the pencil, who does not feel
a secret pride in the honour reflected on the discerning liberality of his country? Such books may be considered as typogra-
phical pictures by eminent artists. Pictures however are not
necessary for the closet of a student! but they may adorn the
museums of a nation or an university, and dignify the reposi-
tories of the opulent and patrician literati. Atticus is magnifi-
cent in such patronage, though Rutilus may incur some censure. This is a noble and a laudable use of the superfluity of
wealth. It is also political in the highest degree. In times like
these men of talents and genius, when unemployed and let loose
upon the world, become too frequently the pests of society and
the canker worms of the community.—It is indeed high time
to awake out of sleep, and to discern the peculiar use of every
blessing. In all our actions, we should have a view to the stability of society and of well-regulated government. It becomes
us all to observe and separate the essential and unvarying laws
of order from the principles of confusion, and the dictates of
sound sense from the wildness of ungoverned fancy and of presumptuous intellect; that the grand end and aim may at last be
effected, that we may, by choice and conviction, turn from
lying vanities to the spirit of truth and of life.

‡ Every man has reprobated the *manner* of printing *the glossy* account of
the British Embassy to China, as published by Sir George Staunton, in 4to;
and the public has not forgotten the *unreasonable* demand upon them *in the
increased price,* in open violation of the original agreement and proposal. Was
it for this, Sir George, that the E. I. Company gave THREE THOUSAND
POUNDS for the plates! I shall at present say nothing of the work as a
composition.

O.C T A V.I U.S.

Here close the strain: and o'er your studious hour
May truth preside and virtue's holiest pow'r! 610
Still be your knowledge temp'rate and *(e)* discreet,
Though not as Jones sublime, as Bryant great;

T 2

Pre-

(e) The advice of Octavius is good, but not applicable to a
man so insignificant as his friend.—But to men of knowledge
and of ability in every department of life it is of deep importance. I lament and am indignant, when I think of such a scholar as Dr. Parr, and the waste of erudition and talents. Let
him stand for a genius. The want of discretion and prudence
has ruined more men of learning and genius than the time would
allow me to mention. Without this sobriety of intellect nothing is strong, nothing is great. Without this prudence, without a discernment of time and circumstance, and *the habit of regularity*, without an attention to the decencies, of society, and of
common life and of the principles by which all men, however
gifted, *must* indiscriminately be conducted, all our attainments are nothing worth. They will never procure us esteem or respectability among men. The world will but smile
at such scholars; and ministers, when called upon to promote
them, will tell you not, without reason, "*they are not producible.*"*
Let me give two passages on this subject, one from Milton,
the other from Dr. Johnson, variously applicable and of deepest
consequence.

> "He who reads
> Incessantly, and to his reading brings not
> A spirit and judgment equal or superior,
> Uncertain and unsettled still remains,
> Deep vers'd in books, and shallow in himself,
> Crude or intoxicate, collecting toys,
> As children gathering pebbles on the shore."

P. R. b. 4. v. 322.

To

* The words of the Duke of Newcastle on such an occasion, when he was
Prime Minister in George the Second's reign. They were spoken of a man,
whose genius, talents, eloquence and erudition honoured and supported the
Church of England. And he was not promoted.

Prepar'd to prove in Senate, or the Hall,

That states by learning rise, by learning fall ;

Serene, not senseless, through the awful storm,   615

In principle sedate, to shun (*f*) Reform ;

To

To men of genius (as at leaſt they are called) Dr. Johnson gave this ſolemn admonition: " This relation (of the life of Sa-vage) will not be wholly without it's use, if those who, in con-fidence of ſuperior capacities or attainments, *disregard the com-* " *mon maxims of life,* shall be reminded *that nothing will supply* " *the want of prudence,* and that negligence and irregularity, " long continued, will make *knowledge useless, wit ridiculous, and* " *genius contemptible.*" Dr. Johnson's Life of Savage, at the conclusion.

> " Deign on the passing world to cast thine eyes,
> · " *And pause awhile from letters,* TO BE WISE."

(*f*) No factions ever proceeded *to attempt* A REVOLUTION *in any country,* but first under the pretence and through the Me-dium of A REFORM. We have been told with effrontery and with falshood, that the Constitution of England exists only in the imagination ; yet we may read the Bill of Rights. The fact is this. Modern framers of political constitutions will never be satisfied, till they are laid down like the elements of mathema-tics in the manner of Euclid. Definitions, Axioms, Postu-lates, primary propositions, subsequent propositions, built upon and proved by the preceding, with corollaries and deductions. One strange writer, (perhaps it is the first time the reader ever heard of him) says, " A CONSTITUTION must be produced *intire and at the same time,* it *must* be simple in it's construction, " and PERFECT *in all it's parts.*" Malkin's Essays on Civiliza-tion, 8vo. (1795) p. 122. I had fondly thought that Lord

Bacon

To mark man's intellect, it's strength. and bound,

              Nor

Bacon had distinguished the works of nature from thofe of art, in that masterly and memorable sentence, " Natura omnium partium rudimenta *simul* parit et procreat." (De Augm. Scient.) I suppose a political Constitution is the work of human art. Indeed if Mr. Malkin were describing a *perfect* poem, epic or tragic, he could not have expressed himself more critically. Yet thus it is, that *our* prefent theoretical writers sport with man and his passions. They certainly confider *us all* as passive machines, and *they apply their laws,* with as much cool indifference to their fellow creatures, and with as little feeling, as they would *apply the axe* or any mechanical instrument to lop a tree or to raise a weight. Their systems uniformly proceed on this principle. They never vary. Mercy is not in all their thoughts; there is neither allowance for human frailty, nor revision of judgment. Man has offended : he *muft* die the death. " Gnossius hæc Rhadamanthus habet DURISSIMA REGNA." We have all seen and felt, *what* the revolutionary principle *is*. We muft never for a moment forget, that the object of France, from her *firft* revolution, has been and is *to change the government in every state in Europe* and in every part of the world which she can pervade. or influence. Look in Germany, in Belgium, in Italy, in Spain, in the isles of the Eaftern or of the Weftern Archipelago; caft your view, broad and unrestrained, from the dominions of the Porte to the banks of the Ohio or the Missisippi, not a state, not a fortress, not a work, not a fragment of nature or of art, not a cliff, not a torrent, not a precipice, but has felt the shock and impulse of revolutionary terror. *Abyssus abyssum invocat !* One deep has called upon another, the winds have blown the signal of encounter, and the cataracts are roaring and conflicting; or in the resounding language of the poet of Panopolis †,

Συνερχομενων νεφεων μυκητορι ρομβω
Βρονται*η* *ζ*αρυδ*υ*πος ε*ζ*ομ*ζ*εεν ομ*ζ*ριος ηχω !

† Nonnus, Dionys. Lib. 41. v. 84. p. 1059. Edit. Hanov. 1610.

Nor deem stability on change to found ;

To

I must claim excuse and indulgence for my expressions. My mind is either borne down or hurried away with the terrors of impending desolation, and the overthrow or confusion of fixed, regulated, established government. My sensations are solitary; but they are deep. Την ψυχην μ8 διερχεται Ρομφαια. I have indeed the consolation of affectionate and honourable friendship, and I am not without the approval of a few who are wife and good : but I cannot say that " in my life time I have had too much of noise and compliment.‡" I have risen. in silence; and in peace and privacy it is my desire to set and to depart. But can any of us see what we have seen, and not labour to avert it from our own country? If I could conceive a being of lefs political significance than myself, I would call even on him for assistance. *The object, the undiverted object of France is* THE OVERTHROW OF ENGLAND ! NOS NOSTRAQUE, the form of our government, the fundamental laws, and the principles by which property is *acknowledged and secured.* These have been attacked by assault, by storm, by breach, by sedition, by the arms of ribaldry, of obscenity, of blasphemy. At one time they open upon us the floodgates of treason and madness, at another they sap the foundation by a circuitous stream winding and working unperceived. *They know* that a Revolution can alone be effected *by a Reform.* There is no other mode. A state may prove bankrupt; but a revolution is not the necessary consequence of bankruptcy. I view with fear the finances of Great Britain, but not without a rational hope of final though tardy restoration. The proposal of Reform is my specific apprehension. The proposers of Reform, such as Mr. Pitt formerly and Mr. Grey at present, I

firmly

‡ An expression in the affecting Will of the Rt. H. Edmund Burke. What declaration, what testimony, what experience will *convince* us of the " Vera bona atque illis multum diversa, remota erroris nebula ?"

. To feel with Mirabeau that " Words are (g) Things,"

While

firmly believe are without bad intentions. . But I would esist.them both. . I confess I never could understand the great Lord Chatham's celebrated expression of " infusing a portion of *new*-health into the constitution to enable it to bear it's infirmities." Junius (in his very last letter) calls it " brilliant and full of intrinfic wisdom." For my own part, I think it but false glitter and full of intrinsic nonsense, when applied politically. It is mere rage of metaphor. It is to call the mind a sheet of white paper, till at last we are brought to think the resemblance to be the very thing signified. The use of metaphor is to illustrate, not to prove. But we are always cheating and deluding ourselves. Government, take it in any of it's complex forms, can be carried on but in three ways: by unsullied principle and undeviating virtue in the Governors and perhaps in the people; by force and terror; or by mitigated law and influence. Who does not wish for the first? who expects to see it? In states highly civilized, the mixed mode of law and influence on the minds of free agents appears to me the only mode in which tranquillity, security, and general happiness can be tolerably preserved, with the allowance of human frailty. I detest corruption, open or secret, as much as any man. But when I see an assembly formed on any principles however sublime, or deep, or disinterested, I remember it is formed of men. Menander said long ago; Ανθρωπος! ἱκανη προφασις. It is man; his name explains the reft. I never will consent to think, that Government is a matter of perpetual experiment. Graft new regulations upon the old principles by a gradual removal of what is absurd, obsolete, useless, or an incumbrance. It was the boast of Citizen Lord Stanhope, that he would teach the Judges law, and the Bishops religion. I have no such ambition : but at present I would recommend to Charles Abbott Esq. M.P. the new *Digester* of our Laws, not to be too subtle in the process.

It

While in Delusion's ear their magic rings,   620

                                     Through

It is not every political chemist who can throw off into his work the spirit of legislation, unmingled with the grosser dregs and feculence of the mass. Caution is not timidity. Let us *now* and at all times be vigilant with determinate courage. We know *what* freedom, *what equality of power among the citizens*, what fraternity, what comfort, what happiness and what security France has offered, and *given* too, to all countries, who have either bowed voluntarily, or have been subjected, to her tyranny. Take Cicero's expressions. As to themselves; *Licet, quod vide-* " *tur, publicum judicare; quod judicaverint, vendere.*" As to other nations, friend or foe; "*Perspici non potest, utrum severitas acerbior, an benignitas quæstuosior sit.*" Such are the words in that elaborate and consummate Oration *on the Agrarian Law*, which every man would do well to read and consider in the original or in a translation. It is peculiarly pertinent to the present time. When Demosthenes raised his mighty voice against a decree proposed by one Aristocrates, he bespoke the attention of his audience as to a private man, who had neither part in the administration of the state nor influence from his connections. He bespoke their favour on *this* ground. He thought the interest of Athens was alone a sufficient plea. " Επειδαν εχι των ενοχλυντων ύμας, ὺδε των πε πολιτευμενων και πιστευομενων παρ'ὑμιν ὡν, πραγμα τηλικυτον φημι δειξειν πεπραγμενον."†
For my own part *without any other pretension*, political or literary, than the love I feel to my country, her laws, her ordinances, and her government, and the labour I have exerted to understand and to preserve them, I would remind my Countrymen in this perilous and pressing hour, of the eloquent words of Demonax, as they are recorded by Lucian; " *Consti-* " *tutions and doctrines like these you never will decree, till you have* " *first removed or overthrown* THE ALTAR OF MERCY!" The

                                      words

† Κατα Αριστοκρατυς.— Demosth. Op. Gr. Ed. Benen. 1570.
P. 403.

Through states, or armies, in the camp, or street,

U   And

words of the original are full of dignity: Μη προτερον, ω Αθηναιοι, ψηφισεσθε, αν μη τϑ ΕΛΕΟΥ τον ϛωμον καθελητε. Lucian Demonax. p. 555. Fol. Bourdelotii.

(g) A celebrated saying of the famous Mirabeau, in the beginning of the French Revolution.—I would, in this concluding
note, observe with great earnestness and affection to my country, that in all the departments of society, government, religion,
or literature, the French have all times maintained *one unvarying
system of deception,* when under the ancient monarchy, or *now* under
the iron tyranny of their new republic.' Their manner of reasoning is, and always has been, sophistical. We are in perpetual danger of being mifled by the appearance of reason. We
have always ground for distrust. Take a specimen from thousands and tens of thousands of instances. Many years ago, in
a collection entitled " Lettres Historiques et Politiques,"
a *French* Statesman used these words to Mr. D'Alembert. " Je
" ne veux point *admettre* dans les *arrets* de Conseil *un vrai trivial,*
" une clarté *trop familiere.* Je veux *un vrai de recherche,* une
" clarté elegante, une näiveté fine, *toute brillante de termes pom-*
" *peux,* relevés *inopinément* de phrases arrondies, *de vocatifs in-*
" *termediaires* et *d'adverbes indéfinis.*"   Lett. Hist. et Polit. Vol.
4. p. 176. Nothing can be more characteristic of French Statesmen. Be but sufficiently *unintelligible,* have but your *vocatifs
intermediaires* et your *adverbes indéfinis,* and the business is done.
Language without meaning, phrases to blind the people, and
ideas to delude. But when the scheme is accomplished, *and
when they obtain the power,* their language is perfectly intelligible.
—Next take an instance in literature. Men of learning have
always had a proper value for the *Greek* language, for reasons
too obvious for me to state. In general the French are ignorant

PART IV.   of

And now a school revolts, and now A FLEET.

Go,

of it. Indeed Mr. *Camus (the Deputy)* some time ago published an edition of Aristotle Περι Ζωων, moderate enough as I thought from a slight inspection. But in general the French Philosophers, who by their works prepared the Revolution, are perpetually despising or ridiculing the Greek language. I only speak of their *manner* of effecting their purpose. One of the acutest and most insidious of them all, Mr. D'Alembert, has these words. " *Ah, si vous saviez le Grec !*—Ceux qui sçavent, *ou croient savoir,* l' *Hebreu,* l'*Arabe,* le *Syriaque,* le *Cophte* ou le *Copte* (as if he cared how it was pronounced,) le *Persan,* ou le *Chinois,* pensent et parlent *de même* et *par les memes raisons.*" D'Alembert Melanges de Literature et de Philosophie. Vol. 5. p. 526. We see, the *French* Philosopher by *confounding* the *Arabic, Coptic, Syriac* and *Chinese* with the *Greek,* insinuates that there is an *equal use* in them all, that is, to the *generality* of scholars and to the world at large, *little or no use* at all. This does not merit any answer; but we see the nature of a French Philosopher's proof and the manner of his argument. In short, he either knows every thing, or there is no manner of use at all in any thing that he does not know. Q. E. D. I think from continued observation, I understand the nature of these men. Their literature, their politics, their philosophy, all terminate in the same point. " *Croyez Moi,*" are the words, whether they speak to an individual, or to the nations of the universe.—*Now,* since the Revolution, *from reasoning* they have betaken themselves *to single words.* Deception still. Mirabeau said true, " Words are things." I cannot help observing that the Athenians (whose government was popular, and *consequently tyrannical,* and manured with the blood of her own *citizens*) had a custom of softening the

Go, warn in solemn accents bold and brief,

U 2　　　　　　　　The

the appellation of things which naturally conveyed an idea of terror. This may be found in a most curious extract, preserved by the very learned Photius from the 4th book of the *Chrestomathia* of HELLADIUS BESANTINOUS ; the words are these.,

" Το μη δυσφημα λεγειν πασι τοις Παλαιοις φροντις ην, μαλιστα " δε τοις Αθηναιοις· διο και το Δεσμωτηριον οικημα εκαλην, και " τον Δημιον Κοινον, τας δε Εριννυας σεμνας θεας· κτλ." Photii Bibliothec. Sect. 279. pag. 1593. Edit. 1653. In the same manner the French apply the terms *Equality, Liberty, Fraternity,* &c. for Tyranny, Desolation, Oppression and Plunder. This is well understood. It would be presumption to enlarge on this subject to a kingdom so enlightened, so dignified, and I may add *so prepared* as Great Britain. We have every thing to lose. We have, under our own form of government, comfort, protection, honour, security, and happiness. The price of preserving them is indeed great, very great; but the price of anarchy, reform, and *inextricable* confusion, would be greater beyond all calculation. We have a foe powerful and perhaps unrelenting. But all states yield at last to circumstances ; and policy will grant what affection would refuse. The most ardent wish of my heart is A SECURE PEACE, after a war for ever to be deplored, bloody, fatal, and expensive beyond all example ; but which I always believed, and still believe, to have been INEVITABLE. We have *still* many and great Resources ; but the times never called with so loud and so commanding a voice for wisdom, discernment, and integrity, for temperate, and timely, and *gradual* concession with dignity and security, and for an œconomy rigid and undeviating, *on the part of our governors*; and for obedience, acquiescence under temporary pressure, alacrity in defence, and vigilance, and loyalty, and STEADINESS *in all the subjects of this land.* We have no need

of

The slumb'ring Minister, or factious Chief,

. Mourn

of the Roman † *Armilustrium* ; our arms are -purified already.
Our Soldiers are loyal, and honourable, and without spot. They
have been weighed in the balance, and found perfect. And I
trust our naval flag will never again wave but in defiance *to our*
enemies. We are not lost, if we continue firm. We must remember that all the leagues of French Factions and their Leaders, in England or in any country, never relent. They know not
the meaning of the term. There is as much mercy in them, to use
the phrase of Shakspeare, *as there is milk in a male Tiger.* If they
are called upon to retract, or to declare their full purpose, or to
render their reasons to the country, they give us manifestos and
declarations from their clubs. They tell us of corruption, and reform, and all the sophisms of anarchy and revolution. So thundered the Orator of Athens against such men: "Αντι τε αποδυναι,
σοφισματα ευρισκεσι, και παραγραφας, και προφασεις, πονηροτατοι
ανθρωπων και αδικωτατοι." * But Justice has her balance, and
the sword is not borne in vain. " *At home* (I take the words
" of Sir John Finch in the 4th of Charles I.) *at any rate* AUTHO-
" RITY MUST BE VINDICATED *from contempt*, SINCE THE LIFE OF
" GOVERNMENT IS REPUTATION." And we should remember, that
" None are so bold as the factious in company, none so fearful
" apart." We may have good hope, for we have a good cause.
When perhaps the greatest statesman and the greatest orator
that ever headed an opposition, demands an audience of his Sovereign, I would willingly suppose, that the principle of his heart *is*
not democratic: though I think his principles *in general*, are very dangerous at this time. I would hope we may yet be redeemed. It was the

boast

---

† See Varro de Ling. Lat. Lib. 5. 3. for the word and the illustration of it.
Festus also may be consulted.

* Vid Demosthen. Orat. Προς την Λακριτε παραγραφην.—Dem.
Ed. Gr. Renenati 1570. p. 546. Why will not our Statesmen *study* De-
mosthenes ? Is he not allowed to be the very first *political* Orator ? Mr.
Fox virtually understands his *manner* better than any man in England.
He does not exert it for the same good end.

Mourn proudest empires prostrate in the dust, 625

Tiaras,

boast of the Roman Emperor Augustus, that he found the City of
brick, and left it of marble. I trust we shall not reverse this memorable saying. I trust that *the public credit* of the nation will revive,
and that *in this respect*, when speaking of Mr. P*ITT*, it will not be
engraven with an iron pen and in the rock of England for ever,
" *Auream* invenit, *chartaceam* reliquit." I think I can discern
the firm establishment of lawful constitutional power in the
plunges of meditated convulsion; and the return of day in the
moment of greatest obscuration. I have loved my country
from my earliest years, from a conviction of the excellence of
the Constitution and of that balanced liberty it was formed to
maintain. I am grateful for the protection and the blessings
it has afforded, and is yet mighty to preserve.—I am *again*,
(much against my will, and I sincerely apologize for re-
peating the subject,) *finally* called upon to declare, with
solemnity and with that truth which I have ever 're-
vered and preserved, that this whole composition, verse and
pros e, is the work of *one* hand. In this assertion I have
no mental reservation. I never wore the weeds of Do-
minic, or drank from the cup of Loyola. If this declaration will
not suffice, I shall leave the sable birds of detraction to the
hoa rseness of their own clamours and to the worms on which
they feed. I shall soar upward to the source and fountain of
light. It is also frequently insinuated and sometimes boldly
asserted, to be written *in conjunction* with many learned and
eloquent friends in the groves and retreats of our beloved *Aca-
deme*. It is true indeed, " By the waters of *Cam* I have sat
" down and wept, when I remembered thee, O Sion! as for my
" harp, I have often hanged it up among the trees that are
" therein." I wished to " sing one of the songs of Sion." But,
as it seems, it is an honourable *Conspiracy*, a *Conspiracy* to vindicate,

Tiaras, fanes, and pontiffs, crown and bust,

And

cate, to recommend, and to uphold the cause of government, of Christian religion, of learning, and of good manners! Would it were so! Such united talents might do their perfect work. I have only to lament the unworthiness of him who has presumed, without assistance or co-operation, to undertake that office ALONE ;

> " *To intermit no watch*
> AGAINST THE WAKEFUL FOE, and wide abroad
> *Through all the coasts of dark destruction* SEEK
> DELIVERANCE FOR US ALL!"

If indeed I had either personal hope or personal fear in the political or in the literary world, I think it will be allowed that I should not have published this work. He must reconcile contradictions who will dispute this assertion. Whom have I courted? to whom have I bowed? I am no tory. Arbitrary power in any shape is my abhorrence. I have walked in the school of Locke, and have passed through that of Sidney. But I have, in this hour of maturest reflection, approved and held fast the tempered doctrines which uphold government and prevent confusion. In the political matters of *this* time, my suit and service is not rendered *personally* to Mr. Pitt. *Upon me* HE *can have no claim.* My service is to my Country, and my praise to the Minister of the Crown of Great Britain. My praise is to HIM, who by deliberate and undaunted firmness, with an unblenched dignity, by commanding powers in speech and argument, and by vigorous measures, though without that promptitude of decision which marked his great Father, has preserved and supported (long may he preserve and support them!) the principle and stability of the English government and constitution. *The main voice of England goes with me in this.* Such I esteem Mr. PITT: as such I honour him. *Am I his enemy?* I see his errors and his vices too, and I lay no flattering unction to them. I am alive to all his public virtues,

and

And last, as through the smould'ring flames you turn,

                           .   '   Snatch

and I would correct their aberrations, for they are many. As to Mr. Fox; that he has not discerned the signs of these times, I will not assert: but *that* his imprudence, his unbridled licence of language, and his plunging desperate doctrines in times like these in and out of Parliament, have alienated the mind of his Country *from Him*, that I will maintain. If I were to give credence to *all* his speeches which I have either heard or read, I must declare them to be the doctrines of a man ripe and ready for *any* revolution. If he is honest in his opinion, I can neither think nor pronounce him honest to his country. He should not have *thus* exhibited himself in the House or on the Hustings. *Non hæc ista sibi tempus spectacula po.cit!* I pass over the primrose path of dalliance on St. A :

the no⁻ʲ

der he

tuous

the lᴏ᷄

his genius, to his political eloquence without an equal, to his knowledge various, deep, and extensive. His pleasantry, his social friendly disposition, and the good temper of his private conversation are acknowledged. But if he is ever to direct the councils of this kingdom, he must tread back *almost all* his steps. If he turns to o̅u̅r government, *he must be born again*. With opinions bold and candid as these I might obtain some respect and perhaps some attention from the public, but I could hardly please either Mr. Pitt or Mr. Fox. If I sought personal fame; my motive is still more visionary. No man can account for it. He who loved fame best* said of it, " Just what you hear you have." I am wholly unknown. It is very proper that I should be so. Yet I would be understood even on this point. I have not the sacred fear of a coward, but the deliberate

                                        courage.

* Mr. Pope.

Snatch THE PALLADIUM, though the Temple
burn. 628

courage which is inspired by reflection, and the confidence
which I am proud to repose in honourable friendship. Some
literary and political enterprizes are indeed rather hazardous in
their nature. Mine are of that number. Yet I love decorum and
I would be guided by discretion; but it is not the form only of
those virtues, refined through certain strainers, that I would
preserve, it is the spirit. I would have gentleness without timidity, and decision without presumption. But I *must* feel the
pressing nature of the time, the burthens, the terrors, the perils,
and the necessity OF THE STATE. Whoever would do a public
service, must forget himself. His remuneration is from within.
As to myself, however unavailing my actions, my sentiments,
my abilities, or my services, they are UNKNOWN, UNBOUGHT,
UNSOLICITED, *and shall be* UNALTERED. In spirit, in principle, and in affection, my words and my thoughts are these:

> *Non ante revellar*
> *Exanimem quam te complectar* ROMA, *tuumque*
> *Nomen,* LIBERTAS, *et inanem prosequar umbram!* *

* Lucan. L. 2. v. 301.

August 1797.

THE END.

www.ingramcontent.com/pod-product-compliance
Lightning Source LLC
Chambersburg PA
CBHW021126020726
47500CB00003B/939